DAY HIKES AROUND
LOS ANGELES

45 GREAT HIKES

by Robert Stone

D1495299

Day Hike Books, Inc.
RED LODGE, MONTANA

Published by Day Hike Books, Inc.
P.O. Box 865
Red Lodge, Montana 59068

Distributed by The Globe Pequot Press
246 Goose Lane
P.O. Box 480
Guilford, CT 06437-0480
800-243-0495 (direct order) · 800-820-2329 (fax order)
www.globe-pequot.com

Photographs by Robert Stone
Design by Paula Doherty

The author has made every attempt to provide
accurate information in this book. The author and publisher do
not assume any responsibility for loss, damage or injury caused
through the use of this book. Please let this book guide you,
but be aware that each hiker assumes responsibility
for their own safety.

Cover photo: Newton Canyon Falls, Hike 6
Back cover photo: Chicken Ridge Bridge
above Rustic Canyon, Hike 31

Table of Contents

THE HIKES

Malibu to Santa Monica

Hollywood Hills and Griffith Park

About the Hikes

Despite the imminent presence of the Los Angeles metropolis, the surrounding area is comprised of hundreds of acres of natural, undeveloped land with numerous out-of-the-way hiking trails. From the coast to the interior mountains and valleys, there are several diverse and distinct ecosystems providing homes to many species of animals.

This guide will take you to 45 outstanding hikes around Los Angeles, getting you to the trailhead and onto the trail with clear, concise directions. Most of these hikes are found in the foothills, canyons, and peaks of the Santa Monica Mountains, a range running parallel to the coast from Los Angeles to Point Mugu. Highlights of the hikes include numerous panoramic views from the ocean to the city, unusual geological formations and rock outcroppings, bluffs, waterfalls, ridge walks, canyons, old ranch roads (including Ronald Reagan's ranch), filming locations, and cool shady retreats. You may see several different species of wildlife, perhaps one of the few mountain lions still living in the region.

These hikes are often located in beautiful park and picnic areas which can be enjoyed for the whole day. To help you decide which hikes are most appealing to you, a brief summary of the highlights is included with each hike.

The trailheads are found within a short drive of Los Angeles. Each of the hikes is accompanied with its own trail map and detailed driving and hiking directions. In addition, overall maps of the 45 hikes are found on pages 8—11. Major access roads are presented on these maps. Each hike also lists U.S.G.S. maps and other supplementary maps, which are not necessary but may be interesting for some areas. The hiker who wishes to further explore the Santa Monica Mountains may wish to purchase the newly updated Trails Illustrated map and Hileman's Recreational and Geological Map of Griffith Park.

Be sure to bring drinking water and sunscreen, and be prepared for ticks and poison ivy.

Santa Monica Mountains—Coastal Region
map on pages 8–9

The Santa Monica Mountains extend roughly 46 miles east and west along the Pacific coastline from Los Angeles to Point Mugu. This range of mountains lying along the San Andreas Fault is 8—12 miles wide. The highest point is 3,111 feet at Volcanic Sandstone Peak.

The first 33 hikes in this guide are found in the Santa Monica Mountains between Interstate 405 and the Ventura County line. This region holds the largest number of state parks and natural, undeveloped acres in the mountain range. A large sector of the land was established as the Santa Monica Mountains National Recreation Area in 1978. The trails here meander along the coastal foothills, traverse peaks and ridges, and drop down across the northern side of the range facing into the rolling landscape of interior California.

Large state parks, lush canyons, geological formations, waterfalls, and filming locations are a few of the highlights. Beaches and coastal communities are scattered along the Pacific Coast Highway, the access road to most of these hikes.

The mountain's most well-known trail is the Backbone Trail, which extends approximately 55 miles across ridges and canyons on a nearly continuous trail. When complete, the Backbone Trail will extend 70 miles, linking the Santa Monica Mountains from east to west.

You will enjoy the smells of sage, evergreens, and seawater as you explore the canyons and peaks of the Santa Monica Mountains.

Hollywood Hills and Griffith Park
map on pages 10–11

Hollywood Hills and Griffith Park are located at the east end of the Santa Monica Mountain Range. Griffith Park, the largest municipal park in the United States, has both tourist attractions and solitary retreats within its 4,100 acres. It contains a 53-mile network of hiking and equestrian trails through the semiarid foothills and wooded glens. The mountains and steep interior canyons of the Hollywood Hills are largely undeveloped and offer a haven for humans and animals in the midst of the Los Angeles metropolis.

This guide includes eleven hikes in Hollywood Hills and Griffith Park. This cross-section of hikes offers an excellent sampling of the plant life, terrain, and incredible views of the area. Highlights include overlooks of the city, secluded canyons, gardens, the Hollywood Reservoir, Griffith Park Observatory and Planetarium, a 1926 merry-go-round, and a hike up to the famous "HOLLYWOOD" sign. Several other local attractions are within easy access from many of the trailheads, including the Los Angeles Zoo, Gene Autry Western Heritage Museum, Travel Town Museum, and five golf courses.

Although all of the hikes in this guide are accessible and enjoyable year-round, they are often more beautiful in late winter through spring when the streams are active and the foliage is lush green. Wear comfortable hiking shoes, and bring sunscreen, protective clothing, and drinking water.

Hiking in the hills and mountains around Los Angeles will give you an appreciation of the open country surrounding this metropolitan area. Enjoy your day hike as you discover greater Los Angeles out on the trails!

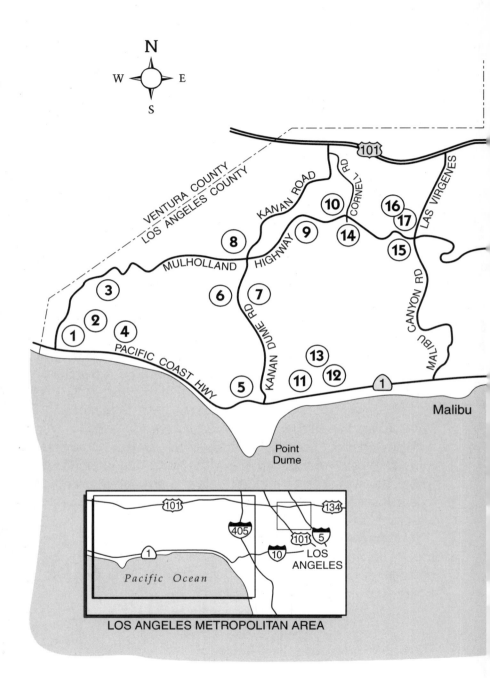

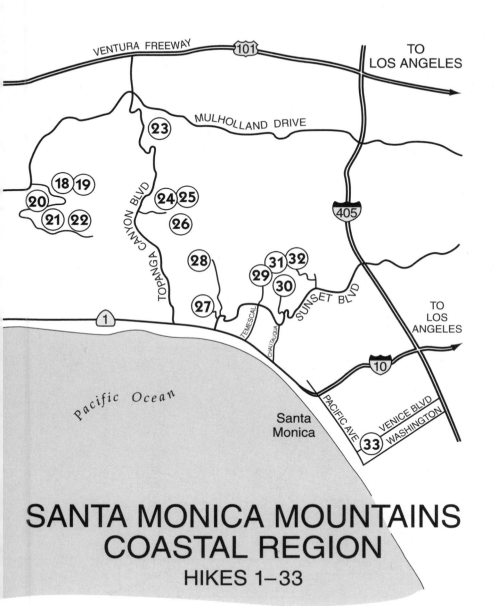

SANTA MONICA MOUNTAINS COASTAL REGION
HIKES 1–33

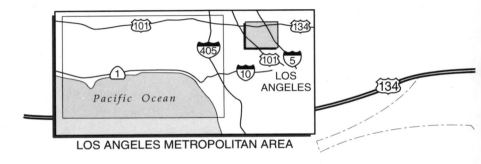

LOS ANGELES METROPOLITAN AREA

HOLLYWOOD HILLS AND GRIFFITH PARK
HIKES 34–45

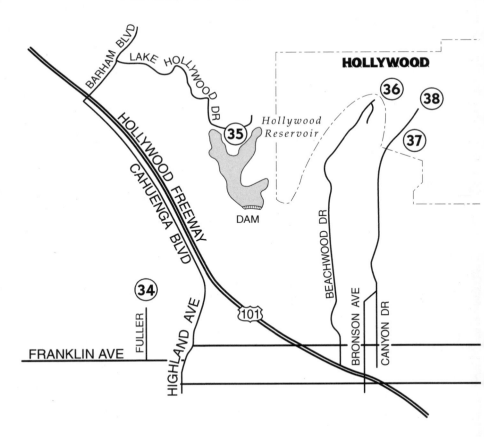

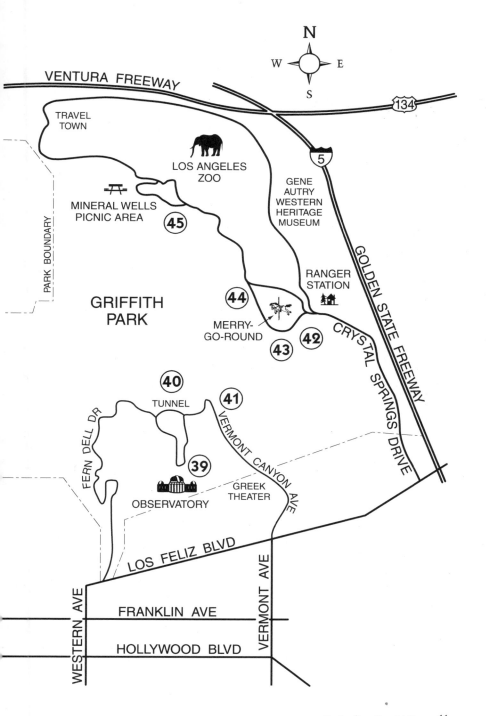

Hike 1
Nicholas Flat and Willow Creek Trails
Leo Carrillo State Park

Hiking distance: 2.5-mile loop
Hiking time: 1.3 hours
Elevation gain: 612 feet
Maps: U.S.G.S. Triunfo Pass
Leo Carrillo State Beach map
Trail Map of the Santa Monica Mountains West

Summary of hike: This loop hike in Leo Carrillo State Park leads to Ocean Vista, a 612-foot knoll with great views of the Malibu coastline and Point Dume. The Willow Creek Trail traverses the east-facing hillside up Willow Creek Canyon to Ocean Vista. The hike returns along the Nicholas Flat Trail, one of the few trails connecting the Santa Monica Mountains to the Pacific Ocean.

Driving directions: From Santa Monica, drive northbound on the Pacific Coast Highway to the Leo Carrillo State Park entrance and turn right. The turnoff is 14 miles past Malibu Canyon Road. Park in the day-use parking lot.

Hiking directions: The trailhead is 50 yards outside the park entrance station. Take the signed trail 100 yards northeast to a trail split. The loop begins at this junction. Take the right fork—the Willow Creek Trail—up the hillside and parallel to the ocean, heading east. At a half mile the trail curves north, traversing the hillside while overlooking the arroyo and Willow Creek. Three switchbacks lead aggressively up to a saddle and a signed four-way junction with the Nicholas Flat Trail. The left fork leads a quarter mile to Ocean Vista. After marveling at the views, return to the four-way junction and take the left fork. Head downhill on the Nicholas Flat Trail across the grassy slopes above the park campground. Return to the junction near the trailhead.

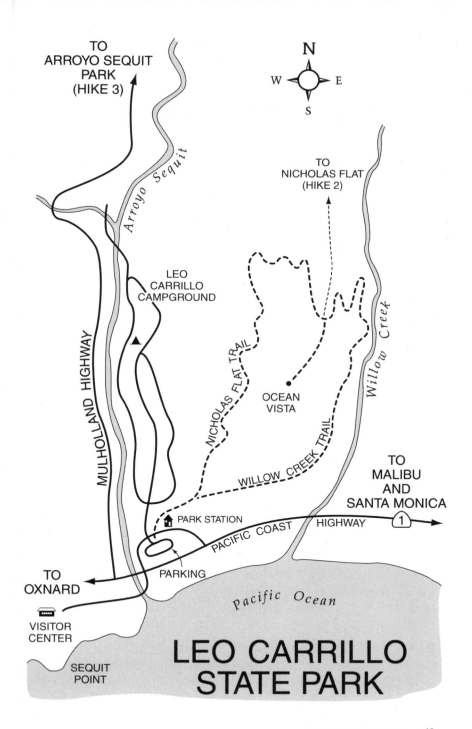

TO
ARROYO SEQUIT
PARK
(HIKE 3)

N
W   E
S

Arroyo Sequit

TO
NICHOLAS FLAT
(HIKE 2)

LEO
CARRILLO
CAMPGROUND

MULHOLLAND HIGHWAY

NICHOLAS FLAT TRAIL

Willow Creek

OCEAN
VISTA

WILLOW CREEK TRAIL

TO
MALIBU
AND
SANTA MONICA

PARK STATION   HIGHWAY   1

PACIFIC COAST

PARKING

TO
OXNARD

VISITOR
CENTER

SEQUIT
POINT

Pacific Ocean

LEO CARRILLO
STATE PARK

Hike 2
Nicholas Flat

Hiking distance: 2.5-mile double loop
Hiking time: 1.3 hours
Elevation gain: 100 feet
Maps: U.S.G.S. Triunfo Pass
       Leo Carrillo State Beach map
       Trail Map of the Santa Monica Mountains West

Summary of hike: Nicholas Flat, located in Leo Carrillo State Park, is a grassy highland meadow with large oak trees, a manmade pond, and rock outcroppings. This hike skirts around Nicholas Flat with spectacular views of the ocean, San Nicholas Canyon, and the surrounding mountains. The Nicholas Flat Trail may be hiked 3.5 miles downhill to the Pacific Ocean, connecting to Hike 1.

Driving directions: From Santa Monica, drive northbound on the Pacific Coast Highway to Decker Canyon Road and turn right. (Decker Canyon Road is 11.8 miles past Malibu Canyon Road.) Continue 2.4 miles north to Decker School Road and turn left. Drive 1.5 miles to the road's end, and park alongside the road.

Hiking directions: Hike south past the metal gate and kiosk. Stay on the wide, oak-lined trail to a junction at 0.3 miles. Take the right fork, beginning the first loop. At 0.6 miles is another junction. Again take the right fork—the Meadows Trail. Continue past the Malibu Springs Trail on the right to Vista Point, where there are great views into the canyons. The trail curves south to a junction with the Nicholas Flat Trail, which leads to Leo Carrillo State Park. Take the left fork around the perimeter of the flat, passing the trail on the right to another Vista Point, and complete the first loop at 1.8 miles. Take the trail to the right at two successive junctions to a pond. Follow the edge of the pond northeast through the meadow, completing the second loop. Return to the trailhead on the wide path.

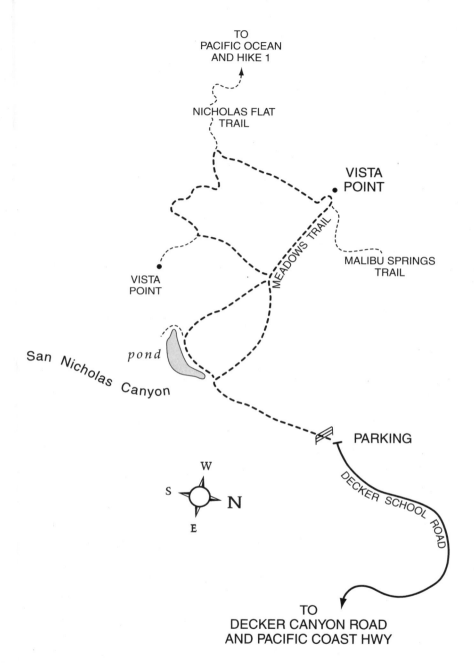

TO
PACIFIC OCEAN
AND HIKE 1

NICHOLAS FLAT
TRAIL

VISTA
POINT

MEADOWS TRAIL

MALIBU SPRINGS
TRAIL

VISTA
POINT

pond

San Nicholas Canyon

PARKING

W

S — N

E

DECKER SCHOOL ROAD

TO
DECKER CANYON ROAD
AND PACIFIC COAST HWY

NICHOLAS FLAT

Hike 3
Arroyo Sequit Park

Hiking distance: 2.5-mile loop
Hiking time: 1.3 hours
Elevation gain: 250 feet
Maps: U.S.G.S. Triunfo Pass
Trail Map of the Santa Monica Mountains West

Summary of hike: Arroyo Sequit Park, a former ranch, takes in 155 acres of open meadows with picnic areas and a canyon. From the meadows are panoramic views of the ocean and surrounding mountains. In the canyon is a seasonal tributary of the East Fork of the Arroyo Sequit and a waterfall.

Driving directions: From Santa Monica, drive northbound on the Pacific Coast Highway to Mulholland Highway and turn right. (Mulholland Highway is 14.2 miles past Malibu Canyon Road.) Continue 5.5 miles up the canyon to the signed turnoff on the right at mailbox 34138. Turn right into the park entrance and park.

Hiking directions: Head south on the park road past the gate, kiosk, and ranch house. At 0.2 miles take the road to the left—past the astronomical observing site and picnic area—to the footpath on the right. Leave the service road on the nature trail, heading south. The trail skirts the east edge of the meadow, then descends into a small canyon and crosses several seasonal stream crossings. Head west along the southern wall of the canyon, passing a waterfall on the left. Cross a wooden footbridge over the stream, and descend to the canyon floor. Continue west, cross the East Fork Arroyo Sequit, and begin the ascent out of the canyon to a junction. Continue straight ahead up the hill. A series of switchbacks lead up the short but steep hill. Once at the top, cross the meadow to the road. Take the service road back to the parking area.

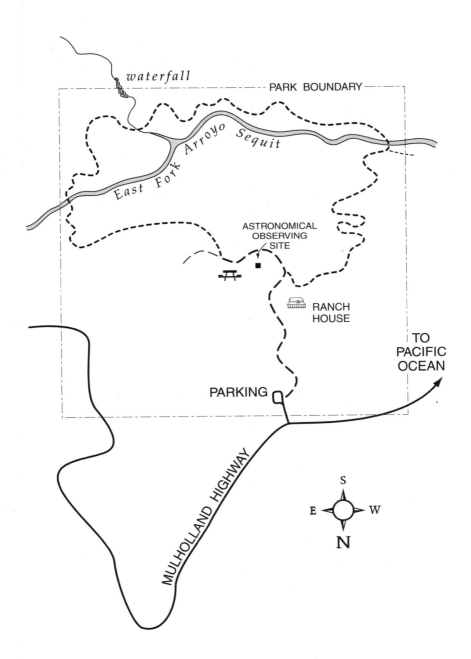

waterfall

PARK BOUNDARY

East Fork Arroyo Sequit

ASTRONOMICAL
OBSERVING
SITE

RANCH
HOUSE

TO
PACIFIC
OCEAN

PARKING

MULHOLLAND HIGHWAY

S

E W

N

ARROYO SEQUIT PARK

Hike 4
Charmlee Park

Hiking distance: 3-mile loop
Hiking time: 1.5 hours
Elevation gain: 600 feet
Maps: U.S.G.S. Triunfo Pass
City of Malibu—Charmlee Natural Area map
Trail Map of the Santa Monica Mountains West

Summary of hike: Charmlee Park has a network of interconnecting trails throughout its 460 acres. Most of the park trails are old ranch roads. The trails cross grassy rolling meadows, passing oak groves, rock outcroppings, and several ocean overlooks along the 1,250-foot bluffs. The park has several picnic areas and a nature center.

Driving directions: From Santa Monica, drive northbound on the Pacific Coast Highway to Encinal Canyon Road and turn right. (Encinal Canyon Road is 11.2 miles past Malibu Canyon Road.) Continue 3.7 miles to the park entrance on the left. Drive 0.2 miles on the park road to the parking lot.

Hiking directions: Hike past the information board and picnic area on the wide trail. Pass a second picnic area on the left in an oak grove, and continue uphill to a three-way trail split. The middle trail is a short detour leading to an overlook set among rock formations and an old house foundation. Take the main trail to the left into the large grassy meadow. Two trails cross the meadow and rejoin at the south end—the main trail heads through the meadow while the right fork skirts the meadow's western edge. At the far end is an ocean overlook and a trail fork. Bear left past an old ranch reservoir. Continue downhill, curving north through an oak grove to the unsigned Botany Trail, a narrow footpath on the right. The Botany Trail winds back to the picnic area and the trailhead.

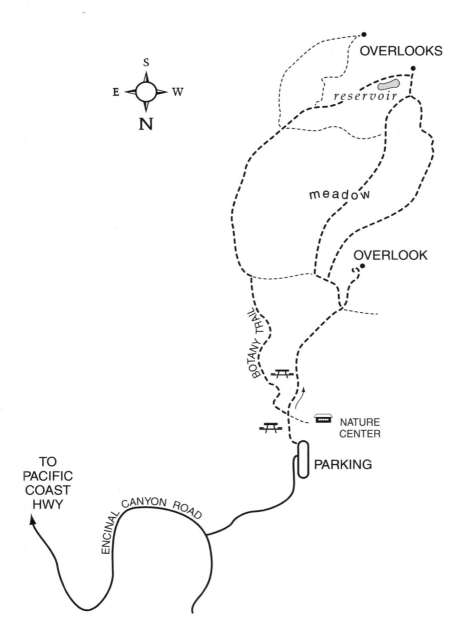

CHARMLEE PARK

Hike 5
Lower Zuma Canyon

Hiking distance: 1.7-mile loop
Hiking time: 1 hour
Elevation gain: 250 feet
Maps: U.S.G.S. Point Dume
　　　　Trail Map of the Santa Monica Mountains Central

Summary of hike: Zuma Canyon is one of the few canyons in the Santa Monica Mountains that is accessible only to foot and horse traffic. There are no paved roads. This hike begins on the Zuma Canyon Trail. The trail heads up the drainage parallel to Zuma Creek past lush riparian vegetation, oak, willow, and sycamore trees. The hike returns on the Zuma Loop Trail above the canyon floor, traversing the hillside overlooking the canyon and the ocean.

Driving directions: From Santa Monica, drive northbound on the Pacific Coast Highway to Bonsall Drive and turn right. (The turnoff is one mile past Kanan Dume Road.) Continue one mile north to the trailhead parking area at road's end. The last 200 yards are on an unpaved lane.

Hiking directions: From the end of the road, hike north past the trailhead gate on the Zuma Canyon Trail. At 0.2 miles is a junction with the Zuma Loop Trail. Go straight on the Zuma Canyon Trail past oak and sycamore trees. Continue past the junction with the Ocean View Trail on the right, cross Zuma Creek, and head to a junction with the Canyon View Trail. Bear left, remaining close to the creek. At 0.7 miles, cross Zuma Creek to a junction. To add an additional 1.4 miles to the hike, take the right fork 0.7 miles up the canyon, crossing the creek several times to the trail's end. Return to the junction, and take the Zuma Loop Trail to the west, traversing the hillside. Follow the ridge south, bearing left at three separate trail forks before returning down to the canyon floor and completing the loop. Take the right fork back to the trailhead.

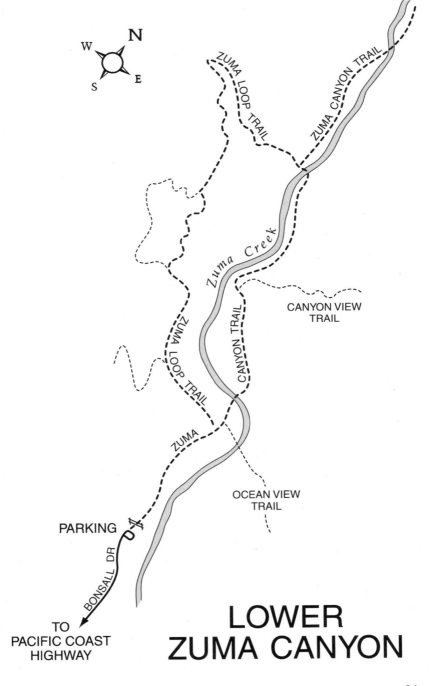

N
W · E
S

ZUMA LOOP TRAIL

ZUMA CANYON TRAIL

Zuma Creek

CANYON VIEW
TRAIL

ZUMA LOOP TRAIL

CANYON TRAIL

ZUMA

OCEAN VIEW
TRAIL

PARKING

BONSALL DR

TO
PACIFIC COAST
HIGHWAY

LOWER
ZUMA CANYON

Hike 6
Upper Zuma Canyon
Newton Canyon Falls

Hiking distance: 1.5 miles round trip
Hiking time: 1 hour
Elevation gain: 200 feet
Maps: U.S.G.S. Point Dume
　　　　Trail Map of the Santa Monica Mountains Central

Summary of hike: The Upper Zuma Canyon Trail begins in Newton Canyon. The trail leads a short distance along a portion of the Backbone Trail to Newton Canyon Falls, a beautiful waterfall in a lush, forested grotto with moss-covered rocks (cover photo). There are large, shaded boulders to sit on near the falls by cascading Newton Creek.

Driving directions: From the Ventura Freeway/101 in Agoura Hills, exit on Kanan Road. Head 7.9 miles south to the trailhead parking lot on the right. The parking lot is located just before entering the third tunnel (T-1). (Kanan Road becomes Kanan Dume Road after it crosses Mulholland Highway.)
　　From the Pacific Coast Highway, drive northbound and turn right on Kanan Dume Road (5.8 miles past Malibu Canyon Road). Drive 4.4 miles to the trailhead on the left, just past the tunnel.

Hiking directions: Hike west, away from Kanan Dume Road, on the signed Backbone Trail. The trail immediately begins its descent into the shady canyon. After crossing a trickling stream, a side trail on the left leads 20 yards to the top of the falls. The main trail continues 100 yards downhill to a second cutoff trail on the left. Take this steep side path downhill to Newton Creek, bearing to the left on the way down. Once at the creek, hike upstream along the path. Fifty yards ahead is the lush grotto at the base of Newton Canyon Falls. The main trail continues west into Zuma Canyon and ends at private property alongside Zuma Creek. After enjoying the waterfall, return by retracing your steps.

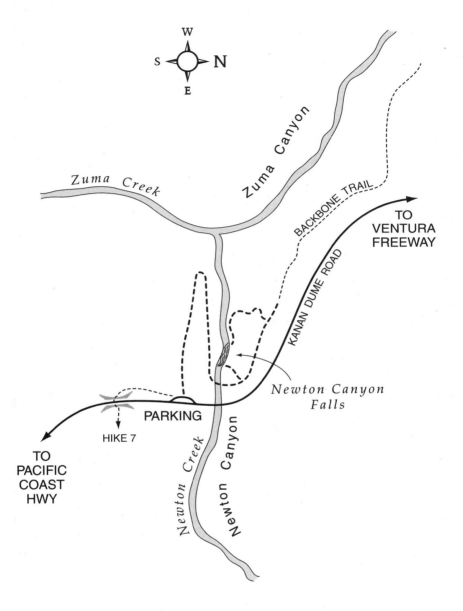

W

S ✦ N

E

Zuma Creek

Zuma Canyon

Zuma Canyon

BACKBONE TRAIL

TO
VENTURA
FREEWAY

KANAN DUME ROAD

Newton Canyon
Falls

PARKING

HIKE 7

TO
PACIFIC
COAST
HWY

Newton Creek

Newton Canyon

UPPER
ZUMA CANYON

Hike 7
Newton Canyon

Hiking distance: 5 miles round trip
Hiking time: 2.5 hours
Elevation gain: 300 feet
Maps: U.S.G.S. Point Dume
Trail Map of the Santa Monica Mountains Central

Summary of hike: This hike overlooks Newton Canyon along the Backbone Trail between Kanan Road and Latigo Canyon Road. The forested trail winds along the ridge of a dense, oak-filled canyon with ocean views and seasonal stream crossings.

Driving directions: From the Ventura Freeway/101 in Agoura Hills, exit on Kanan Road. Head 7.9 miles south to the trailhead parking lot on the right. The parking lot is located just before entering the third tunnel (T-1). (Kanan Road becomes Kanan Dume Road after it crosses Mulholland Highway.)
From the Pacific Coast Highway, drive northbound and turn right on Kanan Dume Road (5.8 miles past Malibu Canyon Road). Drive 4.4 miles to the trailhead on the left, just after the tunnel.

Hiking directions: The signed trail begins by Kanan Road and heads south. The trail, an old fire road, climbs up to the tunnel and crosses over Kanan Road. After crossing, the old road narrows to a footpath and enters a forested canopy, slowly descending into the canyon. Along the way, the trail crosses a paved road, then climbs to various overlooks. Continue along the winding mountainside above Newton Canyon. Near the end of the trail, a maze-like series of switchbacks lead to Latigo Canyon Road. This is a good stopping place.
To hike further, cross the road to the trailhead parking area, and continue on the Backbone Trail. It is another 1.4 miles to Castro Crest Motorway. Return to the trailhead the same way you came.

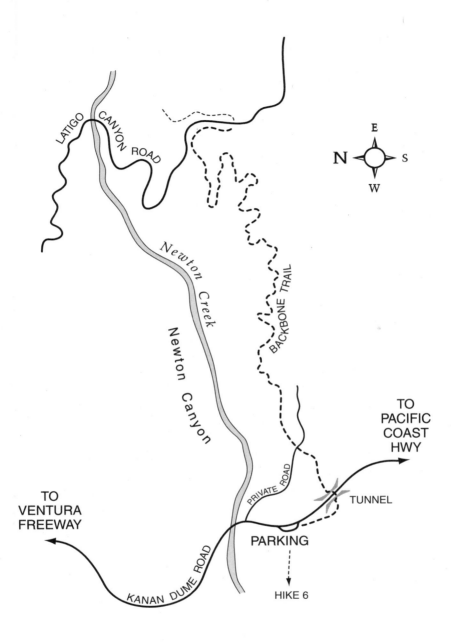

E
N W
S
W

LATIGO CANYON ROAD

Newton Creek

Newton Canyon

BACKBONE TRAIL

TO PACIFIC COAST HWY

PRIVATE ROAD

TO VENTURA FREEWAY

TUNNEL

PARKING

KANAN DUME ROAD

HIKE 6

NEWTON CANYON

Hike 8
Rocky Oaks Park

Hiking distance: 2-mile loop
Hiking time: 1 hour
Elevation gain: 200 feet
Maps: U.S.G.S. Point Dume
      N.P.S. Rocky Oaks Site
      Trail Map of the Santa Monica Mountains Central

Summary of hike: The 200-acre Rocky Oaks Park was once a cattle ranch. The park includes an oak woodland, sage- and chaparral-covered hills, a pond, meadow, scenic overlooks, and picnic areas. This easy loop meanders through the park, visiting each of these diverse ecological communities.

Driving directions: From the Ventura Freeway/101 in Agoura Hills, exit on Kanan Road. Drive 6.1 miles south to Mulholland Highway. Turn right and a quick right again into the Rocky Oaks Park entrance and parking lot.
    From the Pacific Coast Highway, drive northbound and turn right on Kanan Dume Road, located 5.8 miles past Malibu Canyon Road. Drive north to Mulholland Highway and turn left.

Hiking directions: Hike north past the rail fence to the Rocky Oaks Loop Trail, which heads in both directions. Take the left fork a short distance to a four-way junction. Continue straight ahead on the middle path towards the Overlook Trail. Ascend the hillside overlooking the pond, and take the horse-shoe bend to the left. Beyond the bend is the Overlook Trail. This is a short detour on the left to a scenic overlook with panoramic views. Back on the main trail, continue northeast around the ridge, slowly descending to the valley floor near Kanan Road. Bear sharply to the right, heading south to the Pond Trail junction. Both the left and right forks loop around the pond and rejoin at the south end. At the junction, go south and back to the Rocky Oaks Loop, then retrace your steps back to the trailhead.

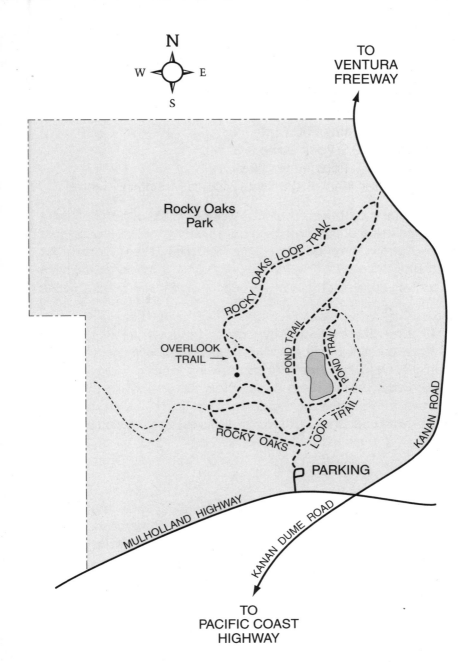

ROCKY OAKS PARK

Hike 9
Peter Strauss Ranch

Hiking distance: 1 mile round trip
Hiking time: 30 minutes
Elevation gain: 200 feet
Maps: U.S.G.S. Point Dume
N.P.S. Peter Strauss Ranch Site
Trail Map of the Santa Monica Mountains Central

Summary of hike: Triunfo Creek flows through the 65-acre Peter Strauss Ranch with picnic areas along the wide creekside lawns. This hike parallels Triunfo Creek and traverses the hillside above the creek through eucalyptus, oak, and sycamore groves. The ranch has an aviary, amphitheater, and a stone house built in 1926.

Driving directions: From the Ventura Freeway/101 in Agoura Hills, exit on Kanan Road. Head 3 miles south to Troutdale Drive. Turn left and drive 0.4 miles to Mulholland Highway. Turn left and immediately turn right into the Peter Strauss Park entrance and parking lot.
From the Pacific Coast Highway, drive northbound and turn right on Malibu Canyon Road. Drive 6.5 miles to Mulholland Highway. Turn left and drive 5.1 miles to the park entrance on the left.

Hiking directions: Take the footpath towards Mulholland Highway and the entry arch. Cross the bridge over Triunfo Creek, and enter the park on the service road to the left across from Troutdale Drive. Head south past the amphitheater to the end of the service road. Stay to the left, parallel to Triunfo Creek. The forested trail traverses the hillside above the creek to a junction. Take the right fork up a series of switchbacks. At the top, the trail levels out and heads west. At the west end, switchbacks lead down the hillside and across a wooden bridge to a junction. The right fork leads to a picnic area. The left fork completes the loop at the amphitheater and aviary.

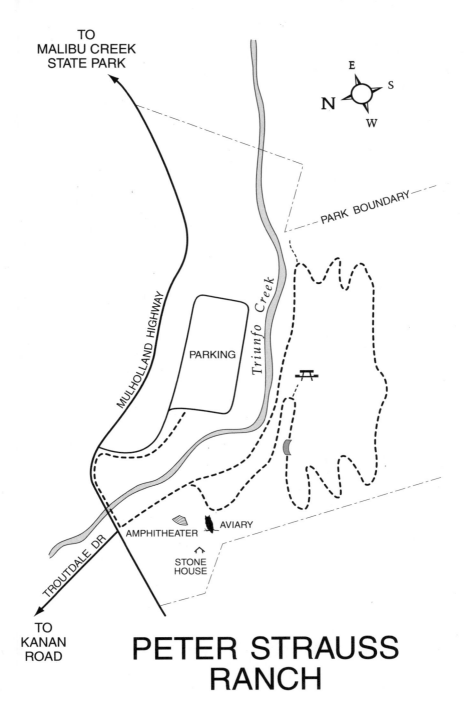

TO
MALIBU CREEK
STATE PARK

E

N ⬩ S

W

PARK BOUNDARY

MULHOLLAND HIGHWAY

PARKING

Triunfo Creek

AMPHITHEATER

AVIARY

STONE
HOUSE

TROUTDALE DR

TO
KANAN
ROAD

PETER STRAUSS RANCH

Hike 10
Paramount Ranch

Hiking distance: 1.75 miles round trip
Hiking time: 1 hour
Elevation gain: 300 feet
Maps: U.S.G.S. Point Dume
       N.P.S. Paramount Ranch Site
       Trail Map of the Santa Monica Mountains Central

Summary of hike: Paramount Ranch has oak woodlands, creeks, canyons, and the prominent Sugarloaf Peak. The scenic and diverse landscape has been used in hundreds of movies and television shows, including *Dr. Quinn, Medicine Woman; Have Gun Will Travel; The Rifleman;* and *Tom Sawyer.* There are two loops in this hike. The Coyote Canyon Trail begins by strolling through a western town to the trailhead. The Medea Creek trail parallels the creek near Sugarloaf Peak.

Driving directions: From the Ventura Freeway/101 in Agoura Hills, exit on Kanan Road. Head 0.4 miles south to Cornell Road. Turn left; drive 1.8 miles to the Paramount Ranch entrance. Turn right and continue 0.2 miles to the parking area.
    From the Pacific Coast Highway, drive northbound and turn right on Malibu Canyon Road. Continue 6.5 miles to Mulholland Highway. Turn left and drive 3.2 miles to Cornell Road. Turn right to the ranch entrance on the left.

Hiking directions: COYOTE CANYON TRAIL—0.75 MILE LOOP: Cross the bridge over Medea Creek, and walk through the western town to the signed Coyote Canyon Trail. Head west up the small ravine to a junction. The left fork is the half-mile Overlook Trail. The right fork follows the ridgeline to another junction. The left fork leads to a picnic area, and the right fork heads down to a paved road. Bear to the right and return through the western town.
    MEDEA CREEK AND RUN TRAIL—1 MILE LOOP: From the parking area, head south on the service road parallel to Medea Creek.

Take the signed trail bearing left. Switchbacks lead up to a junction. Continue straight ahead on the Run Trail along the park perimeter to a trail split. Bear left towards Sugarloaf Peak. Curve to the right above the meadow at the base of the mountain. Descend into the wooded area parallel to Medea Creek, returning to the trailhead.

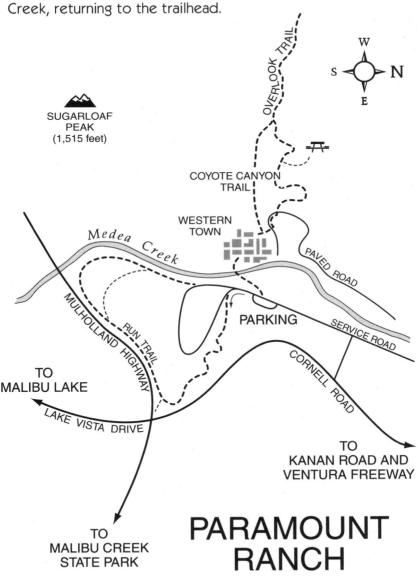

SUGARLOAF
PEAK
(1,515 feet)

OVERLOOK TRAIL

W
S — N
E

COYOTE CANYON
TRAIL

WESTERN
TOWN

Medea Creek

PAVED ROAD

MULHOLLAND HIGHWAY

RUN TRAIL

PARKING

SERVICE ROAD

CORNELL ROAD

TO
MALIBU LAKE

LAKE VISTA DRIVE

TO
KANAN ROAD AND
VENTURA FREEWAY

TO
MALIBU CREEK
STATE PARK

PARAMOUNT RANCH

Hike 11
Escondido Falls

Hiking distance: 4.2 miles round trip
Hiking time: 2 hours
Elevation gain: 300 feet
Maps: U.S.G.S. Point Dume
　　　　Trail Map of the Santa Monica Mountains Central

Summary of hike: Escondido Falls tumbles 50 feet into a shallow pool, cascading off limestone cliffs into a mossy fern grotto. The hike to the falls begins on a winding, paved residential road due to trail access problems. In less than a mile, the trail descends into the forested canyon. In the shade of oaks and sycamores, the canyon trail follows a year-round creek to the waterfall.

Driving directions: From Santa Monica, drive northbound on the Pacific Coast Highway to Winding Way and turn right. Winding Way is 4.5 miles past Malibu Canyon Road. The signed parking lot is on the left side of Winding Way.

Hiking directions: Hike north up Winding Way past some beautiful homes and ocean vistas. At 0.8 miles, leave the road on the well-defined trail, crossing the meadow to the left. Hike downhill into Escondido Canyon and cross the creek. After crossing, take the left fork upstream. (The right fork leads to Latigo Canyon.) Continue up the well-defined, nearly level trail beside the creek. The trail crosses the creek a few more times. After the fifth crossing, Escondido Falls comes into view. The trail ends by the shallow pool at the base of the waterfall. Return by reversing your route.

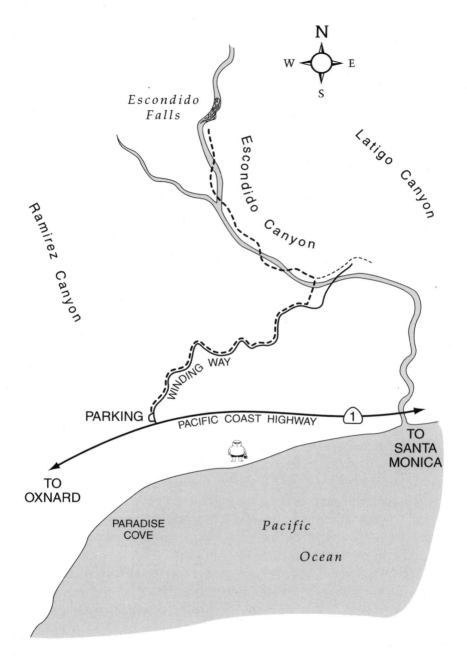

ESCONDIDO FALLS

Hike 12
Dry Canyon Trail to waterfall
Solstice Canyon

Hiking distance: 1.2 miles round trip
Hiking time: 30 minutes
Elevation gain: 200 feet
Maps: U.S.G.S. Malibu Beach
        N.P.S. Solstice Canyon map
        Trail Map of the Santa Monica Mountains Central

Summary of hike: The Dry Canyon Trail is located in Solstice Canyon Park. The trail leads up an oak-filled canyon to an overlook of a seasonal, free-falling waterfall. After a rain, when the fall is active, the long, slender, multi-teared waterfall drops 200 feet off the hillside cliff.

Driving directions: From Santa Monica, drive northbound on the Pacific Coast Highway to Corral Canyon Road and turn right. Corral Canyon Road is 2.3 miles past Malibu Canyon Road. Continue 0.2 miles to the gated entrance on the left. Turn left, entering the park, and drive 0.3 miles to the parking lot at road's end.

Hiking directions: From the parking area, hike 20 yards back down the road to the signed Dry Canyon Trail on the left. Head north up the side canyon into a grassy oak tree grove. The well-defined trail parallels and crosses the creek. As you near the falls, the trail gains more elevation. The falls is across the narrow canyon on the left. This is our turnaround spot. Return along the same path.

To hike further, the trail continues a short distance to the end of the canyon before switchbacks lead up the canyon wall outside the park boundary. Beyond the waterfall, the trail becomes overgrown with brush and faint.

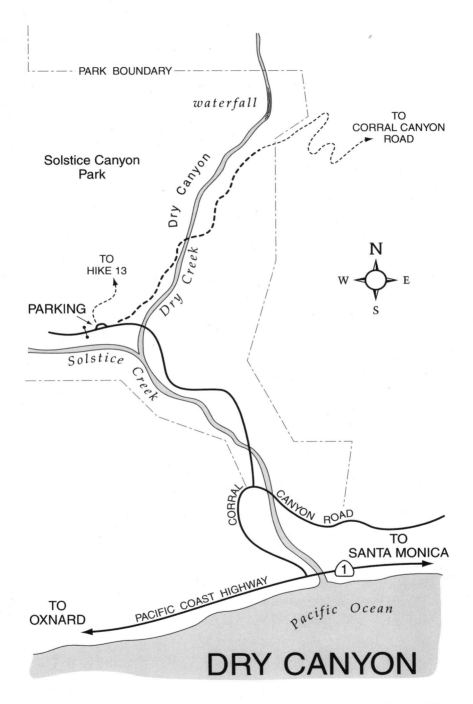

PARK BOUNDARY

waterfall

Solstice Canyon
Park

Dry Canyon

Dry Creek

TO
HIKE 13

PARKING

Solstice Creek

TO
CORRAL CANYON
ROAD

N
W   E
S

CORRAL CANYON ROAD

TO
SANTA MONICA

1

PACIFIC COAST HIGHWAY

TO
OXNARD

Pacific Ocean

DRY CANYON

Hike 13
Solstice Canyon Falls

Hiking distance: 2.8-mile loop
Hiking time: 1.5 hours
Elevation gain: 400 feet
Maps: U.S.G.S. Point Dume and Malibu Beach
      N.P.S. Solstice Canyon map
      Trail Map of the Santa Monica Mountains Central

Summary of hike: The hike up Solstice Canyon leads to Tropical Terrace, the ruins of a home built in the 1950s and destroyed by fire in 1982. The stone courtyard, garden terraces, stairways, and exotic tropical plants still remain. Near the ruins is Solstice Canyon Falls cascading 30 feet over sandstone rocks. The hike up canyon on the Rising Sun Trail traverses the cliffs overlooking Solstice Canyon and the Pacific Ocean. The return route parallels Solstice Creek.

Driving directions: From Santa Monica, drive northbound on the Pacific Coast Highway to Corral Canyon Road and turn right. Corral Canyon Road is 2.3 miles past Malibu Canyon Road. Continue 0.2 miles to the gated entrance on the left. Turn left and drive 0.3 miles to the parking lot at road's end.

Hiking directions: Hike north up the steps past the TRW Trailhead sign. Wind up the hillside to a service road. Take the road uphill to the right to the TRW buildings, now home for the Santa Monica Mountains Conservancy. The Rising Sun Trail begins to the right of the second building. Long, wide switchbacks lead up to the east ridge of Solstice Canyon. Follow the ridge north towards the back of the canyon, and descend through lush vegetation. At the canyon floor, cross the creek to the ruins. Take the path upstream to the waterfalls and pools. After exploring, return on the service road parallel to Solstice Creek. A half mile down canyon is the Keller House, a stone cottage built in 1865. Bear left at a road split, cross a wooden bridge, and return to the trailhead.

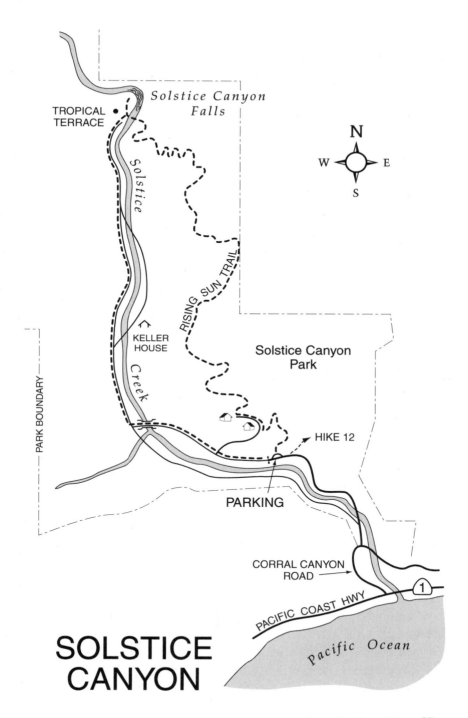

TROPICAL
TERRACE

Solstice Canyon
Falls

Solstice

N
W · E
S

RISING SUN TRAIL

KELLER
HOUSE

Creek

Solstice Canyon
Park

HIKE 12

PARKING

PARK BOUNDARY

CORRAL CANYON
ROAD

PACIFIC COAST HWY

1

Pacific Ocean

SOLSTICE
CANYON

Hike 14
Reagan Ranch Trail
Malibu Creek State Park

Hiking distance: 3 miles round trip
Hiking time: 1.5 hours
Elevation gain: Level hiking
Maps: U.S.G.S. Malibu Beach
Malibu Creek State Park Map

Summary of hike: This ranch was President Ronald Reagan's home in the 1950s and 1960s before he was elected governor of California. It now occupies the northwest corner of Malibu Creek State Park. This state park is host to a variety of outdoor activities, such as camping, fishing, horseback riding, and hiking. It is also home to many animals, including mountain lion, bobcat, coyote, deer, raccoon, snake, lizard, golden eagle, heron, and duck. The Reagan Ranch trails include a duck pond, a large rolling meadow, oak tree groves, stream crossings, magnificent views, and a visit to the Reagan barn.

Driving directions: From Santa Monica, drive north on the Pacific Coast Highway for 13 miles to Malibu Canyon Road. Turn right and continue 6.5 miles up this beautiful winding canyon road to Mulholland Highway. Turn left and drive 3.2 miles to Cornell Road. Turn left again and immediately park along Cornell Road wherever you find a spot.

From the Ventura Freeway/101, exit at the Kanan Road off-ramp. Drive south 0.4 miles to Cornell Road. Turn left and continue 2.2 miles to the intersection of Mulholland Highway. Park along Cornell Road.

Hiking directions: Enter the ranch at a gateway through the white rail fence on the southeast corner of Mulholland Highway and Cornell Road. The unpaved road, lined with eucalyptus trees, leads toward the old Reagan barn 0.25 miles ahead. Continue past the barn to a footpath—the Yearling Trail. The duck pond is on the left. Just beyond the pond is the beginning of the loop. Stay to the left on the Yearling Trail, heading towards the meadow. As you hike through the meadow, there are two side trails on the right that intersect with the Yearling Trail. You may bear right on either trail. They connect with the Deer Leg Trail for the return hike. To return, follow the Deer Leg Trail as it winds past large oak trees and crosses Udell Creek back to the trailhead.

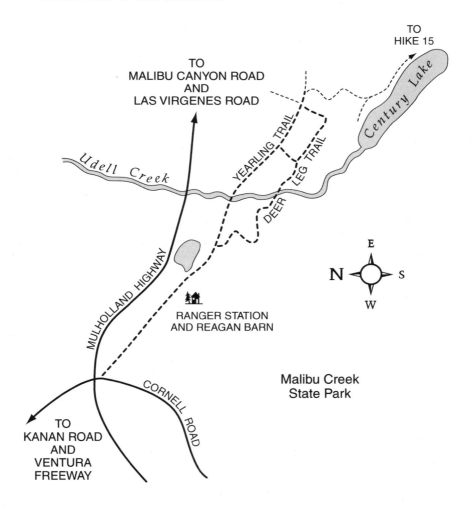

REAGAN RANCH

Hike 15
Rock Pool and Century Lake
Malibu Creek State Park

Hiking distance: 3 miles round trip
Hiking time: 2 hours
Elevation gain: 300 feet
Maps: U.S.G.S. Malibu Beach
   Malibu Creek State Park Map

Summary of hike: Malibu Creek State Park, purchased by the state from the 20th Century Fox movie studio in 1974, was originally home for thousands of years to the Chumash Indians. The park contains a visitor center, campground, a manmade lake, volcanic rock, sandstone outcroppings, majestic canyons, year-round streams, and over 30 miles of hiking trails that spread over its 10,000 acres. This hike follows Malibu Creek to Rock Pool, surrounded by towering volcanic cliffs, and to Century Lake. *Tarzan*, *Planet of the Apes*, and *South Pacific* have been filmed here, to name a few, but it is most recognized for the *M*A*S*H* television series.

Driving directions: From Santa Monica, drive north on the Pacific Coast Highway for 13 miles to Malibu Canyon Road. Turn right and continue 6 miles up the winding canyon road. The state park entrance is located on the left, shortly before reaching Mulholland Highway. Turn left into Malibu Creek State Park. Park in the second parking lot on the left.

From the Ventura Freeway/101, exit at Las Virgenes Road. Head south towards the mountains for 3.5 miles. The state park entrance is located on the right, shortly past Mulholland Highway. Turn right into Malibu Creek State Park.

Hiking directions: Cross the main road to the trailhead. Follow the High Road Trail as it slowly curves alongside Malibu Creek to a bridge heading towards the visitor center. Along the way, you will pass a concrete creek crossing on the left. At the Malibu Creek bridge, take the Gorge Trail to the right.

Bear left along the stream through a lava rock field to Rock Pool, 0.9 miles from the trailhead.

Return to the main trail back at the bridge. Take Crags Road—the main road—to the northwest. Continue uphill to a trail junction at the crest of the hill. From here you will overlook Century Lake and Las Virgenes Valley. The trail to the left leads down to the lake. Continuing right on Crags Road leads to the *M*A*S*H* set. To return, retrace your steps.

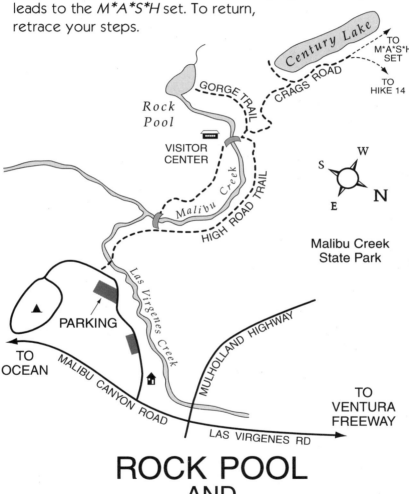

ROCK POOL
AND
CENTURY LAKE

Hike 16
Liberty Canyon
Malibu Creek State Park

Hiking distance: 3.8 miles round trip
Hiking time: 2 hours
Elevation gain: 100 feet
Maps: U.S.G.S. Malibu Beach and Calabasas
Trail Map of the Santa Monica Mountains Central

Summary of hike: Liberty Canyon is one of three natural preserves in Malibu Creek State Park. The canyon has a rare stand of California valley oak. This trail leads up the valley floor to the head of the canyon.

Driving directions: From Santa Monica, drive north on the Pacific Coast Highway for 13 miles to Malibu Canyon Road. Turn right and continue 6.5 miles up this beautiful, winding canyon road to Mulholland Highway. Turn left and park 0.1 mile ahead in the parking pullouts on either side of the road.

From the Ventura Freeway/101, take the Las Virgenes Road exit. Drive 3.1 miles south to Mulholland Highway. Turn right and park 0.1 mile ahead in the parking pullouts.

Hiking directions: Begin on the signed Grasslands Trail, heading north past a white house on the left. Cross the rolling grasslands, looping around the west side of an Edison substation. Continue north past oak trees, bearing right at a trail split. Cross a footbridge over Liberty Creek by a small waterfall and pools to a signed junction. Head left on the Liberty Canyon Trail past a junction at one mile with the Talepop Trail (Hike 17). Continue straight ahead, climbing the hillside through an oak grove overlooking the canyon, and return to the canyon bottom. The trail ends at the head of the canyon by Park Vista Road and Liberty Canyon Road. The Phantom Trail heads southwest to the left. Return along the same trail.

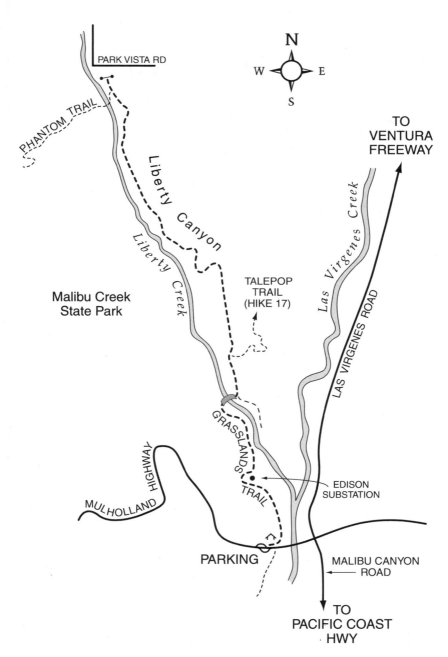

LIBERTY CANYON

Hike 17
Talepop Trail
Malibu Creek State Park

Hiking distance: 4.6 miles round trip
Hiking time: 2.5 hours
Elevation gain: 450 feet
Maps: U.S.G.S. Malibu Beach and Calabasas
　　　Trail Map of the Santa Monica Mountains Central

Summary of hike: This loop hike begins in Liberty Canyon in Malibu Creek State Park. The Talepop Trail climbs to a grassy ridge overlooking two canyons, traverses the ridge, and returns in Las Virgenes Canyon parallel to Las Virgenes Creek. Talepop Trail is named for a small Chumash Indian village.

Driving directions: Follow the driving directions for Hike 16 to the parking pullouts on Mulholland Highway.

Hiking directions: Take the signed Grasslands Trail, and head north across the rolling meadow. Loop around an Edison substation. Continue north, bearing right at a trail split to a footbridge. Cross the bridge over Liberty Creek by rock formations and pools to a signed junction. Take the left fork on the Liberty Canyon Trail, beginning the loop. At one mile is a signed junction with the Talepop Trail on the right. Head west on the Talepop Trail, winding up the west canyon wall to the ridge. Follow the ridge north to the summit, overlooking Liberty Canyon on the west and Las Virgenes Canyon on the east. At the northern park boundary, bear right, down the hillside. Switchbacks lead to the Las Virgenes Canyon floor by Las Virgenes Creek and a junction. Take the right fork along the west side of the creek. As you approach White Oak Farm, take the signed Liberty Canyon Trail to the right. A short distance ahead is a junction, completing the loop. Bear left on the Grasslands Trail, cross the bridge, and retrace your steps.

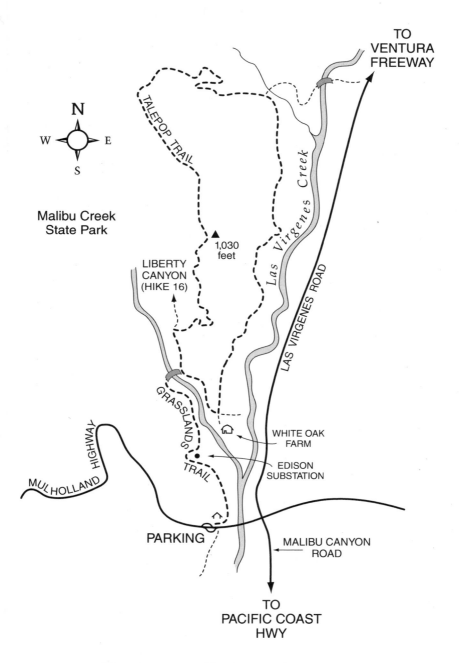

N

W ✦ E

S

Malibu Creek
State Park

TO
VENTURA
FREEWAY

TALEPOP TRAIL

▲ 1,030 feet

LIBERTY
CANYON
(HIKE 16)

Las Virgenes Creek

LAS VIRGENES ROAD

GRASSLANDS TRAIL

WHITE OAK
FARM

EDISON
SUBSTATION

MULHOLLAND HIGHWAY

PARKING

MALIBU CANYON
ROAD

TO
PACIFIC COAST
HWY

TALEPOP TRAIL

Hike 18
Calabasas Peak

Hiking distance: 4 miles round trip
Hiking time: 2 hours
Elevation gain: 900 feet
Maps: U.S.G.S. Malibu Beach
Trail Map of the Santa Monica Mountains Central

Summary of hike: The Calabasas Peak Trail passes great geological formations. There are tilted sandstone slabs with ribs and large, weathered sandstone outcroppings. Along the trail are views into Red Rock Canyon, Cold Creek Canyon, and Old Topanga Canyon.

Driving directions: From the Ventura Freeway/101 in Calabasas, exit on Las Virgenes Road. Head 3 miles south to Mulholland Highway. Turn left and continue 4 miles to Stunt Road. Turn right and drive one mile to the pullout on the right.
From the Pacific Coast Highway, drive northbound and turn right on Malibu Canyon Road. Drive 6.5 miles to Mulholland Highway.

Hiking directions: Walk 20 yards downhill on Stunt Road, heading west to the trailhead across the road. Walk up the unpaved fire road past the gate. The trail zigzags up the mountain to a junction at 0.7 miles. The right fork heads into Red Rock Canyon (Hike 19). Continue straight ahead to the north along the cliff's edge, passing large eroded sandstone slabs while overlooking Red Rock Canyon. As Calabasas Peak comes into view, the trail curves sharply to the right, circling the peak along an eastern ridge. From the ridge are views into Old Topanga Canyon to the northeast. The trail heads gently downhill before a steep descent. Just before the steep descent, watch for a narrow path on the left. Take this side path west up to the chaparral-covered summit. After lingering at the peak, retrace your steps.

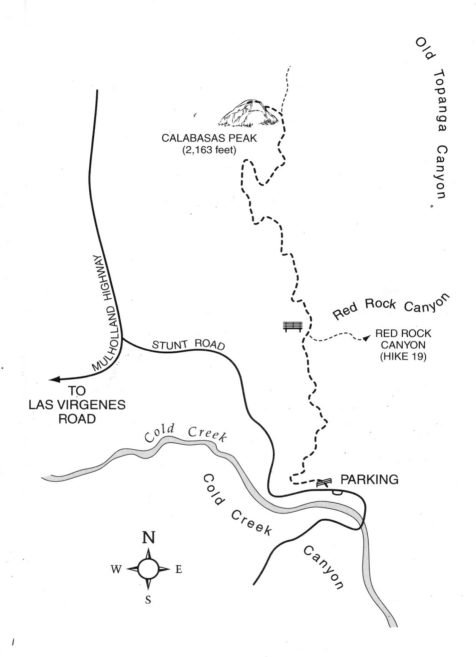

CALABASAS PEAK

Hike 19
Red Rock Canyon

Hiking distance: 4 miles round trip
Hiking time: 2 hours
Elevation gain: 850 feet
Maps: U.S.G.S. Malibu Beach
　　　Trail Map of the Santa Monica Mountains Central

Summary of hike: Red Rock Canyon is a beautiful canyon with large, weather-sculpted sandstone formations. Some of these eroded outcroppings have shallow caves, overhangs, and arches. Shell fossils can be spotted in the rock.

Driving directions: From the Ventura Freeway/101 in Calabasas, exit on Las Virgenes Road. Head 3 miles south to Mulholland Highway. Turn left and continue 4 miles to Stunt Road. Turn right and drive one mile to the pullout on the right.
　　From the Pacific Coast Highway, drive northbound and turn right on Malibu Canyon Road. Drive 6.5 miles to Mulholland Highway.

Hiking directions: Cross Stunt Road and walk 20 yards downhill to the trailhead. Take the unpaved road past the gate, and wind up the mountain. At 0.7 miles is a junction and a bench. The trail straight ahead to the north leads to Calabasas Peak (Hike 18). Take the right fork, heading east into Red Rock Canyon. Continue downhill into the canyon. Pass red sandstone formations to the signed Red Rock Canyon Trail on the left at 1.4 miles. Bear left on the footpath, and walk up wooden steps to the base of some formations. The trail curves up the draw, across a seasonal stream, and past additional sandstone formations. Continue uphill to the trail's end at an overlook. Return along the same path back to the canyon floor. Before returning, take a short detour 200 yards to the left on the main trail to an awesome red rock formation with shallow caves and arches. Return by retracing your steps.

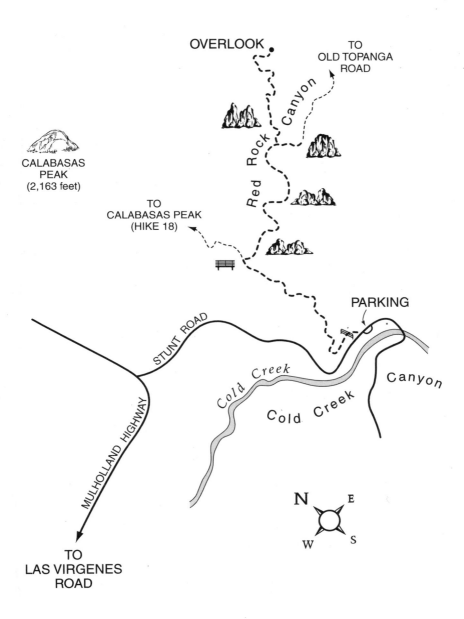

OVERLOOK

TO
OLD TOPANGA
ROAD

Red Rock Canyon

CALABASAS
PEAK
(2,163 feet)

TO
CALABASAS PEAK
(HIKE 18)

PARKING

STUNT ROAD

Cold Creek

Cold Creek Canyon

MULHOLLAND HIGHWAY

N
E
W
S

TO
LAS VIRGENES
ROAD

RED ROCK CANYON

Hike 20
Stunt High Trail

Hiking distance: 3 miles round trip
Hiking time: 1.5 hours
Elevation gain: 300 feet
Maps: U.S.G.S. Malibu Beach
        Trail Map of the Santa Monica Mountains Central

Summary of hike: The Stunt High Trail parallels Cold Creek through riparian woodlands. The trail crosses rolling grasslands up the mountainside, crossing the creek three times en route. This hike follows the lower portion of the trail, staying close to Cold Creek.

Driving directions: From the Ventura Freeway/101 in Calabasas, exit on Las Virgenes Road. Head 3 miles south to Mulholland Highway. Turn left and continue 4 miles to Stunt Road. Turn right and drive one mile to the pullout on the right.
   From the Pacific Coast Highway, drive northbound and turn right on Malibu Canyon Road. Drive 6.5 miles to Mulholland Highway.

Hiking directions: Head southeast, parallel to the road for a short distance. Curve right, away from the road, and cross Cold Creek. Follow the creek downstream into the forested canyon. At 0.5 miles, cross a stream to a junction. Take the right fork, staying close to Cold Creek. (The left fork leads uphill 0.8 miles through open meadows and tree groves to Stunt Road.) The right fork continues northwest high above the creek. At one mile, cross Cold Creek to a junction in the Cold Creek Valley Preserve. Both directions end 0.4 miles ahead. The right fork leads to Stunt Road while the left fork crosses rolling hills to McKain Street, a residential road. Return to the pullout by retracing your steps.

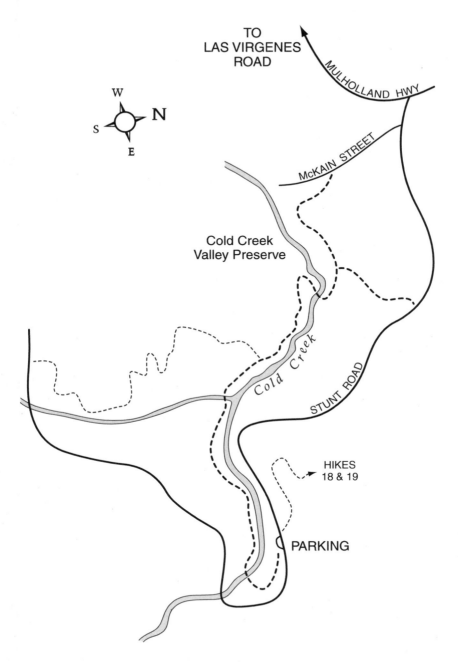

TO
LAS VIRGENES
ROAD

MULHOLLAND HWY

McKAIN STREET

Cold Creek
Valley Preserve

Cold Creek

STUNT ROAD

HIKES
18 & 19

PARKING

W N
S E

STUNT HIGH TRAIL

Hike 21
Cold Creek Canyon Preserve

Hiking distance: 3.2 miles round trip
Hiking time: 1.5 hours
Elevation gain: 800 feet
Maps: U.S.G.S. Malibu Beach
  Trail Map of the Santa Monica Mountains Central

Summary of hike: The 700-acre Cold Creek Canyon Preserve has a lush, creek-fed canyon with small cascades and waterfalls. The trail winds down the canyon through chaparral, maples, bays, sycamores, and oak woodlands. Part of the trail parallels Cold Creek through gardens of ferns with several creek crossings. Watch for the remains of a turn-of-the-century home carved into the giant sandstone boulders.

Driving directions: From the Ventura Freeway/101 in Calabasas, exit on Las Virgenes Road. Head 3 miles south to Mulholland Highway. Turn left and continue 4 miles to Stunt Road. Turn right and drive 3.4 miles to the Cold Creek parking pullout on the left. It is located by a chain link fence.
  From the Pacific Coast Highway, drive northbound and turn right on Malibu Canyon Road. Drive 6.5 miles to Mulholland Highway.

Hiking directions: From the parking pullout, walk through the gate in the chain-link fence, and head east through the tall chaparral. The trail leads downhill along the contours of the hillside and across a wooden bridge over Cold Creek at 0.6 miles. Pass moss-covered rocks and a rusted classic Dodge truck as you make your way into the lush vegetation en route to the canyon floor. Cross Cold Creek again and continue past large sandstone boulders and the remains of the stone house. Several switchbacks lead downhill across streams and past small waterfalls. Due to the storms of 1988, the trail (which used to lead to the lower trailhead gate on Stunt Road) is washed out at 1.6 miles. Return along the same path.

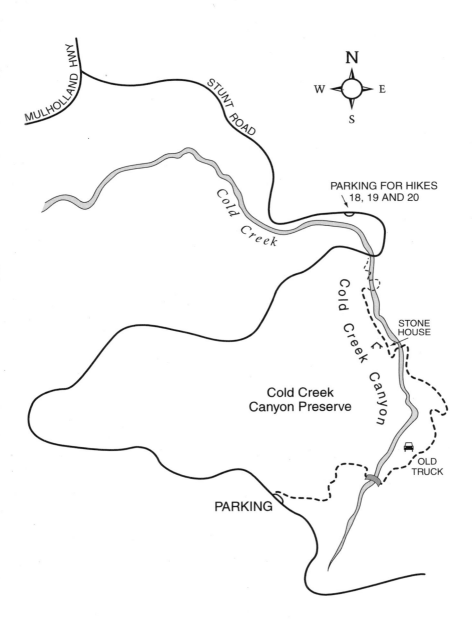

MULHOLLAND HWY

STUNT ROAD

N
W · E
S

Cold Creek

PARKING FOR HIKES
18, 19 AND 20

Cold Creek Canyon

STONE
HOUSE

Cold Creek
Canyon Preserve

OLD
TRUCK

PARKING

COLD CREEK
CANYON PRESERVE

Hike 22
Topanga Ridge to Topanga Lookout
Cold Creek Canyon Preserve

Hiking distance: 2 miles round trip
Hiking time: 1 hour
Elevation gain: 200 feet
Maps: U.S.G.S. Malibu Beach
　　　　 Trail Map of the Santa Monica Mountains Central

Summary of hike: The Topanga Ridge Trail is located in the Cold Creek Canyon Preserve. From this ridge are great views down into Old Topanga Canyon to the east, Cold Creek Canyon Preserve on the west, and the San Fernando Valley into Los Angeles.

Driving directions: From the Ventura Freeway/101 in Calabasas, exit on Las Virgenes Road. Head 3 miles south to Mulholland Highway. Turn left and continue 4 miles to Stunt Road. Turn right and drive 4 miles up the winding road to the end of Stunt Road. Turn left on Saddle Peak Road, and park in the pullout on the right.

　From the Pacific Coast Highway, drive northbound and turn right on Malibu Canyon Road. Drive 6.5 miles to Mulholland Highway.

Hiking directions: From the parking pullout, cross Saddle Peak Road to the gated service road. Head northeast on the paved road, traversing the hillside above Cold Creek Canyon. Calabasas Peak (Hike 18) can be seen to the north. At a quarter mile is a road split. The paved right fork leads to a radar tower. Bear left on the wide, unpaved path and continue gradually uphill. At one mile is a multilevel concrete foundation at the edge of the mountain that overlooks Hondo Canyon, Old Topanga Canyon, the Cold Creek drainage, and the San Fernando Valley into Los Angeles. Return by retracing your steps.

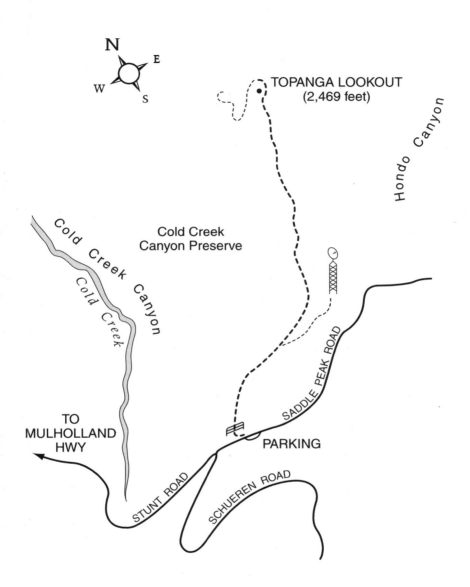

TOPANGA RIDGE
TO THE
LOOKOUT

Hike 23
Summit Valley Trail
Edmund D. Edelman Park

Hiking distance: 2 miles round trip
Hiking time: 1 hour
Elevation gain: 200 feet
Maps: U.S.G.S. Canoga Park
      Trail Map of the Santa Monica Mountains East

Summary of hike: Edmund D. Edelman Park is located in Summit Valley at the head of Topanga Canyon. The 1,500-foot ridge at the north end of this 659-acre park separates rural Topanga Canyon from the urban San Fernando Valley. This hike loops through two valleys, crosses a ridge, and parallels Topanga Creek.

Driving directions: From Santa Monica, drive 4 miles north on the Pacific Coast Highway to Topanga Canyon Boulevard and turn right. Continue 8.2 miles to the signed "Summit Valley/ Edmund D. Edelman Park" parking area on the left.

From the Ventura Freeway/101 in Woodland Hills, exit on Topanga Canyon Boulevard and drive 4 miles south to the parking area on the right.

Hiking directions: Head west past the trailhead gate, and descend into the forested draw. At 0.2 miles is a five-way junction. Take the far right trail—the Summit Valley Canyon Trail—to begin the loop. Head north along the canyon floor parallel to the seasonal Topanga Creek on the right. At one mile, just before descending into a eucalyptus grove, the unsigned Summit Valley Loop Trail bears left. Take this trail as it zigzags up the hillside. Heading south, traverse the edge of the hill to a ridge and a junction. (For a shorter hike, the left fork returns to the five-way junction along the ridge.) Take the middle fork straight ahead, and descend into the next drainage. The trail curves south, returning down the draw to the five-way junction.

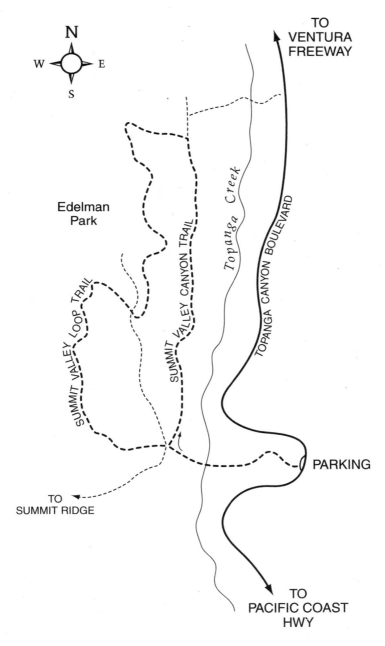

N
W E
S

TO
VENTURA
FREEWAY

Edelman
Park

Topanga Creek

SUMMIT VALLEY CANYON TRAIL

TOPANGA CANYON BOULEVARD

SUMMIT VALLEY LOOP TRAIL

PARKING

TO
SUMMIT RIDGE

TO
PACIFIC COAST
HWY

SUMMIT VALLEY

Hike 24
Dead Horse Trail
Topanga State Park

Hiking distance: 2.5 miles round trip
Hiking time: 1.5 hours
Elevation gain: 400 feet
Maps: U.S.G.S. Topanga
           Trail Map of the Santa Monica Mountains East

Summary of hike: The Dead Horse Trail in Topanga State Park begins in rolling grasslands, enters a riparian forest, and descends into a streamside oak woodland. The trail crosses a wooden bridge over Trippet Creek in a rocky grotto.

Driving directions: From Santa Monica, drive 4 miles north on the Pacific Coast Highway to Topanga Canyon Boulevard and turn right. Continue 4.6 miles to Entrada Road on the right and turn right again. Drive 0.7 miles and turn left, following the posted state park signs. Turn left again in 0.3 miles into the Topanga State Park parking lot.

From the Ventura Freeway/101 in Woodland Hills, exit on Topanga Canyon Boulevard, and drive 7.6 miles south to Entrada Drive. Turn left and follow the posted state park signs to the parking lot.

Hiking directions: Take the signed Musch Trail for 50 yards, heading north to a pond on the right. The Dead Horse Trail heads left (west) across from the pond. The footpath parallels a wood rail fence with rolling grasslands on the right and an oak woodland on the left. At 0.5 miles is a trail split. Take the right fork through chaparral along the contours of the ridge. The trail descends into a shady riparian forest of bay and sycamore trees. A wooden bridge crosses the rocky streambed of Trippet Creek in a narrow draw. After crossing, steps lead up to a junction. Take the middle fork downhill to a trail split. Bear right and loop around to the lower parking lot near Topanga Canyon Boulevard. Return by retracing your steps.

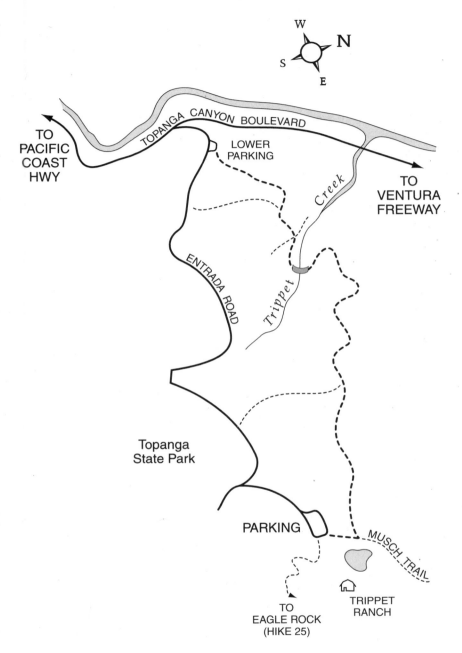

W N
S E

TO
PACIFIC
COAST
HWY

TOPANGA CANYON BOULEVARD

LOWER
PARKING

Creek

TO
VENTURA
FREEWAY

ENTRADA ROAD

Trippet

Topanga
State Park

PARKING

MUSCH TRAIL

TO
EAGLE ROCK
(HIKE 25)

TRIPPET
RANCH

DEAD HORSE TRAIL

Hike 25
Eagle Rock
Topanga State Park

Hiking distance: 4 miles round trip
Hiking time: 2.5 hours
Elevation gain: 800 feet
Maps: U.S.G.S. Topanga
      Trail Map of the Santa Monica Mountains East

Summary of hike: This hike begins at a beautiful picnic area with a pond and a one-mile nature trail in Topanga State Park. The hike follows a fire road up to Eagle Rock, an impressive sandstone rock covered with crevices and caves. The views of the mountains and valleys along this trail, including Santa Ynez Canyon, are superb. The return on the Musch Trail descends past oak, sycamore, and bay trees. This footpath includes lush vegetation, ferns, moss-covered rocks, and stream crossings.

Driving directions: Follow the driving directions for Hike 24 to the Topanga State Park parking lot.

Hiking directions: The trailhead is located at the end of the parking lot by the picnic area. Follow the trail uphill a short distance to a posted junction. Take the left trail—the Santa Ynez Fire Road (also known as Eagle Springs Road). At 0.5 miles along this gradual uphill trail, you will pass the Santa Ynez Canyon Trail on the right. One mile further is the Musch Trail on the left. The trail forks in a short distance. Bear left to Eagle Rock ,which is close and visually prominent.

    From Eagle Rock, return to the Musch Trail junction. Take this footpath to the right as it winds down to the valley through lush foliage and dense oak, sycamore, and laurel woodland. One mile down this trail is a junction at the Musch Camp. Follow the trail sign and walk across the meadow. Turn left a short distance ahead at an unmarked junction and left again at a second unmarked junction. The trail winds back down to the Topanga parking lot, passing a pond along the way.

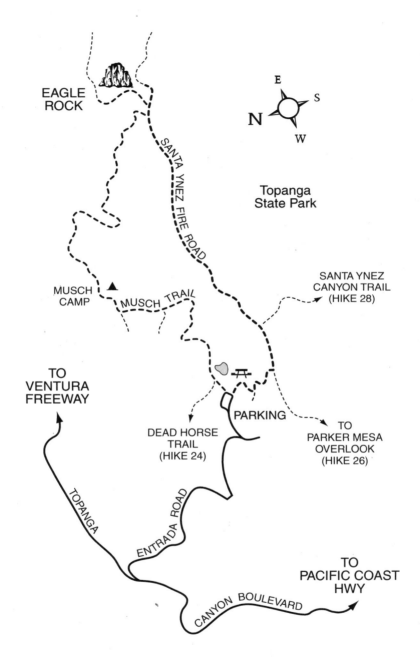

EAGLE
ROCK

E

N · S

W

Topanga
State Park

SANTA YNEZ FIRE ROAD

SANTA YNEZ
CANYON TRAIL
(HIKE 28)

MUSCH
CAMP

MUSCH TRAIL

TO
VENTURA
FREEWAY

PARKING

DEAD HORSE
TRAIL
(HIKE 24)

TO
PARKER MESA
OVERLOOK
(HIKE 26)

TOPANGA

ENTRADA ROAD

TO
PACIFIC COAST
HWY

CANYON BOULEVARD

EAGLE ROCK

Hike 26
Parker Mesa Overlook
from Topanga State Park

Hiking distance: 6 miles round trip
Hiking time: 3 hours
Elevation gain: 800 feet
Maps: U.S.G.S. Topanga
Trail Map of the Santa Monica Mountains East

Summary of hike: This hike follows the Santa Ynez Fire Road (also known as East Topanga Fire Road) along the ridge dividing Topanga Canyon and Santa Ynez Canyon. There are spectacular views into both canyons, including numerous ravines and enormous slabs of sandstone. This hike begins in Topanga State Park and heads south. The trail ends at Parker Mesa Overlook, a barren knoll overlooking the Pacific Ocean. The overlook can also be accessed from the south (Hike 27).

Driving directions: Follow the driving directions for Hike 24 to the Topanga State Park parking lot.

Hiking directions: Head south on the signed trail towards Eagle Rock to a fire road. Bear left up the road to a junction at 0.2 miles. The left fork leads to Eagle Rock (Hike 25). Take the right fork on the Santa Ynez Fire Road past a grove of coastal oaks. Continue uphill to a ridge and a bench with panoramic views of Topanga Canyon to the Pacific Ocean. A short distance ahead, the trail crosses a narrow ridge overlooking Santa Ynez Canyon. Follow the ridge south, with alternating views of both canyons. At 2.5 miles is a junction with a trail on the right. The main trail (left) leads to Paseo Miramar (Hike 27). Leave the main trail, and take the right fork to the Parker Mesa Overlook at trail's end. After enjoying the views, return to the parking area and Trippet Ranch along the same route.

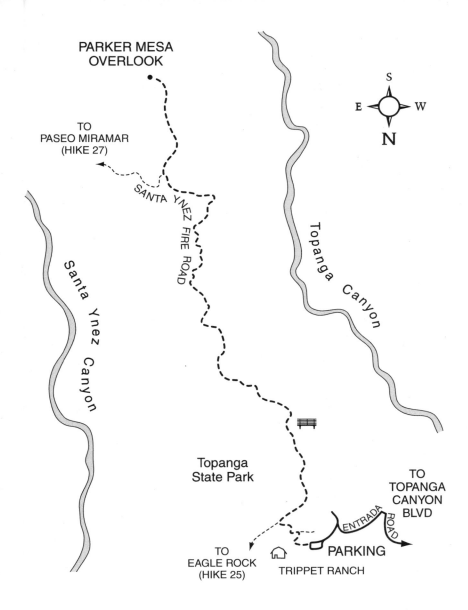

PARKER MESA OVERLOOK
FROM
TOPANGA STATE PARK

Hike 27
Parker Mesa Overlook
from Paseo Miramar

Hiking distance: 5 miles round trip
Hiking time: 2.5 hours
Elevation gain: 1,200 feet
Maps: U.S.G.S. Topanga
       Trail Map of the Santa Monica Mountains East

Summary of hike: The hike to Parker Mesa Overlook from Paseo Miramar has spectacular vistas along the trail. The trail follows the Santa Ynez Fire Road (also known as the East Topanga Fire Road) along a ridge separating Santa Ynez Canyon and Los Liones Canyon. There are views from Venice to Malibu and from West Los Angeles to Topanga. The Parker Mesa Overlook, also known as the Topanga Overlook, is a barren knoll overlooking Santa Monica Bay, Palos Verdes, and on clear days, Catalina Island.

Driving directions: Drive north on the Pacific Coast Highway, and turn right (inland) on Sunset Boulevard. At 0.3 miles, turn left on Paseo Miramar. Drive about one mile to the end of the road and park.

Hiking directions: Hike north past the fire road gate as the road climbs along the ridge. Pass the Los Liones Trail on the left. Continue along the hillside overlooking Santa Ynez Canyon to a junction at two miles. Leave the fire road and take the trail to the left, heading south. The trail ends a half mile ahead at the Parker Mesa Overlook, a bald knoll overlooking the Pacific Ocean. (The main fire road leads three miles further to Trippet Ranch [Hike 26], a park and picnic area in Topanga State Park.) After enjoying the views at the overlook, return along the same trail.

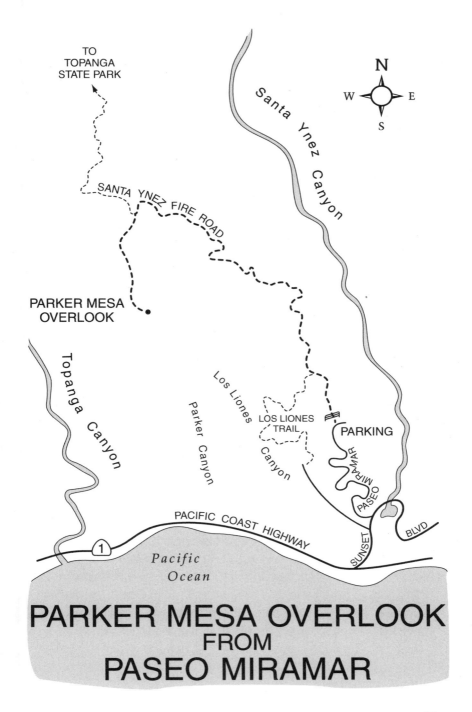

TO
TOPANGA
STATE PARK

N
W   E
S

Santa Ynez Canyon

SANTA YNEZ FIRE ROAD

PARKER MESA
OVERLOOK

Topanga Canyon

Los Liones

Parker Canyon

LOS LIONES
TRAIL

Canyon

PARKING

MIRAMAR

PASEO

PACIFIC COAST HIGHWAY

SUNSET

BLVD

① 1

*Pacific
Ocean*

PARKER MESA OVERLOOK
FROM
PASEO MIRAMAR

Hike 28
Santa Ynez Canyon Trail

Hiking distance: 2.5 miles round trip
Hiking time: 1.5 hours
Elevation gain: 250 feet
Maps: U.S.G.S. Topanga
          Trail Map of the Santa Monica Mountains East

Summary of hike: This trail in Topanga State Park heads up the beautiful Santa Ynez Canyon. The sound of flowing water is constant during the hike as the trail leads to Santa Ynez Canyon Falls, a 15-foot waterfall over sandstone cliffs. The hike includes many creek crossings using rocks as stepping stones. Santa Ynez Canyon is lush, forested, and cool with fern-lined pools and sandstone formations. In the early morning, you may hear the music of croaking frogs.

Driving directions: Drive north on the Pacific Coast Highway to Sunset Boulevard. Turn right (inland) on Sunset, and drive 0.4 miles to Palisades Drive. Turn left on Palisades Drive. Continue 2.4 miles to Vereda de la Montura. Turn left and park at the end of the road a short distance ahead.

Hiking directions: The trail begins on the east bank of the creek and heads up the forested canyon past sycamores, bay laurels, willows, and oaks. At a half mile there is a fork in the trail. The right fork leads up Quarry Canyon. Stay left and cross the creek. Shortly thereafter is a second unsigned fork. Take the trail to the right along the creek, heading north up Santa Ynez Canyon. This trail will lead to the waterfall. (The trail to the left leads 1.5 miles to Trippet Ranch, a picnic and hiking area in Topanga State Park.) As you near the falls, the sandstone cliffs narrow. The trail ends at the back of the canyon in a grotto below the falls. Return by retracing your steps.

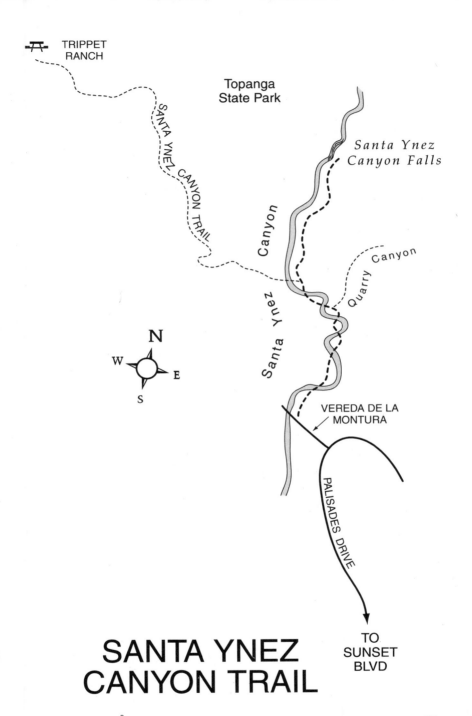

TRIPPET
RANCH

Topanga
State Park

SANTA YNEZ CANYON TRAIL

Santa Ynez
Canyon Falls

Canyon

Quarry Canyon

Santa Ynez

N

W E

S

VEREDA DE LA
MONTURA

PALISADES DRIVE

SANTA YNEZ
CANYON TRAIL

TO
SUNSET
BLVD

Hike 29
Temescal Canyon

Hiking distance: 4-mile loop
Hiking time: 2 hours
Elevation gain: 1,000 feet
Maps: U.S.G.S. Topanga
         Trail Map of the Santa Monica Mountains East

Summary of hike: This loop climbs up a ridge with scenic overviews of the Pacific Ocean and the entire Los Angeles Westside. The trail then descends into Temescal Canyon and returns along the canyon floor. Highlights include a footbridge overlooking Temescal Canyon Falls and Skull Rock, a sandstone outcropping that resembles a human skull.

Driving directions: From Santa Monica, drive north on the Pacific Coast Highway 2.6 miles to Temescal Canyon Road and turn right (inland). Drive to the end of Temescal Canyon Road, crossing Sunset Boulevard, and park at the entrance to the Presbyterian Conference Grounds.

Hiking directions: The signed trail begins at the hiker registration booth on the far end of the parking lot. Head to the left on the Temescal Ridge Trail, climbing the west ridge of the canyon. Several switchbacks take you to the top of the ridge and a junction. A short detour to the left leads a half mile to Skull Rock. After viewing the sandstone formation, return to the main trail. (Watch for the trail on the left.) Head east on the trail as it winds quickly down to the canyon floor, crossing a wooden footbridge at Temescal Canyon Falls. Return on the Temescal Canyon Trail parallel to the creek through the shady forest. Complete the loop back to the parking lot.

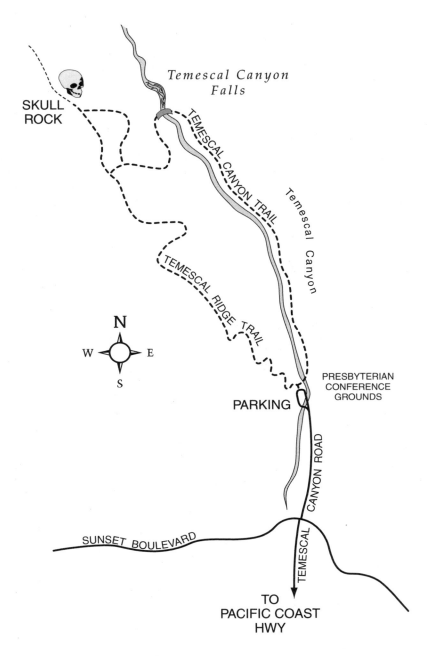

SKULL ROCK

Temescal Canyon Falls

TEMESCAL CANYON TRAIL

Temescal Canyon

TEMESCAL RIDGE TRAIL

N
W E
S

PARKING

PRESBYTERIAN CONFERENCE GROUNDS

TEMESCAL CANYON ROAD

SUNSET BOULEVARD

TEMESCAL

TO PACIFIC COAST HWY

TEMESCAL CANYON

Hike 30
Will Rogers State Park

Hiking distance: 2-mile loop
Hiking time: 1 hour
Elevation gain: 300 feet
Maps: U.S.G.S. Topanga
      Trail Map of the Santa Monica Mountains East

Summary of hike: This hike is a two-mile loop that starts and finishes at Will Rogers' home. The trail overlooks the Los Angeles Basin from downtown to the ocean. At the top of the loop is Inspiration Point, a flat knoll considered the best viewing area of the hike. Picnic grounds, horse riding stables, and daily tours of Will Rogers' house make visiting this state park a wonderful way to spend the day.

Driving directions: From Santa Monica, drive north on the Pacific Coast Highway 1.6 miles to Chautauqua Boulevard and turn right. Continue 0.9 miles to Sunset Boulevard and turn right. Drive 0.5 miles and turn left at Will Rogers State Park. The parking area is 0.7 miles ahead at the end of this road.

Hiking directions: Take the well-maintained trail (a fire road) heading to the left from the visitor center. Near the top of the knoll at 0.8 miles is a signed junction on the right to Inspiration Point. After savoring the views, return to the main loop, and continue north past the signed Backbone Trail on the left. (This is the beginning of the Backbone Trail, which crosses the Santa Monica Mountains for 64 miles to Point Mugu State Park.) The loop continues northeast, then begins its descent to the south, returning to the visitor center. A hiking map is also available at the visitor center that shows other connecting side trails to the main loop.

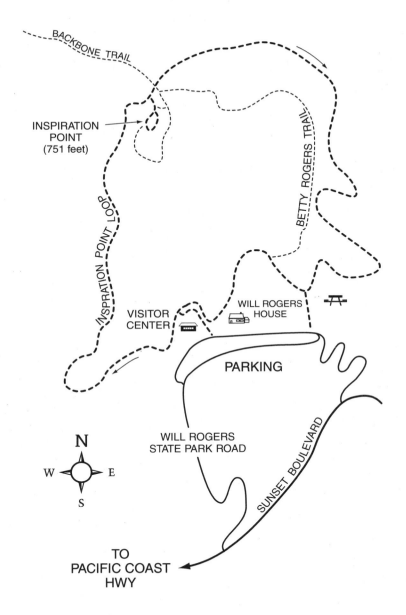

BACKBONE TRAIL

INSPIRATION
POINT
(751 feet)

BETTY ROGERS TRAIL

INSPIRATION POINT LOOP

VISITOR
CENTER

WILL ROGERS
HOUSE

PARKING

WILL ROGERS
STATE PARK ROAD

SUNSET BOULEVARD

N
W   E
S

TO
PACIFIC COAST
HWY

WILL ROGERS
STATE PARK

Hike 31
Rustic Canyon

Hiking distance: 5 miles round trip
Hiking time: 3 hours
Elevation gain: 900 feet
Maps: U.S.G.S. Topanga
      Trail Map of the Santa Monica Mountains East

Summary of hike: This hike follows the Backbone Trail on a ridge between Rustic Canyon and Rivas Canyon. Rustic Canyon lies to the east while Rivas Canyon lies to the west (back cover photo). The first two miles are uphill, but the views are spectacular. A steep descent then leads to the bottom of Rustic Canyon. The hike returns parallel to Rustic Creek through lush vegetation and several old abandoned buildings.

Driving directions: From Santa Monica, drive north on the Pacific Coast Highway 1.6 miles to Chautauqua Boulevard and turn right. Continue 0.9 miles to Sunset Boulevard and turn right. Drive 0.5 miles and turn left at Will Rogers State Park. The parking area is 0.7 miles ahead at the end of this road.

Hiking directions: This hike follows the beginning of the 64-mile Backbone Trail, which runs the length of the Santa Monica Mountains from Will Rogers State Park to Point Mugu.

Take the trail heading left from the visitor center. Continue on this main loop (Hike 30) for approximately one mile to the Backbone Trailhead. The trailhead is just past Inspiration Point and is well marked. Climb north along Chicken Ridge. At 1.5 miles, cross the Chicken Ridge bridge at a saddle that separates Rivas Canyon and Rustic Canyon (back cover photo). Watch for a trail on the right. Leave the Backbone Trail and quickly descend into Rustic Canyon. At the bottom of the canyon, follow the foot trail as it crisscrosses Rustic Creek downstream. The canyon will narrow, then widen out again, leading back to the visitor center. Be careful of poison oak in the narrow part of the canyon.

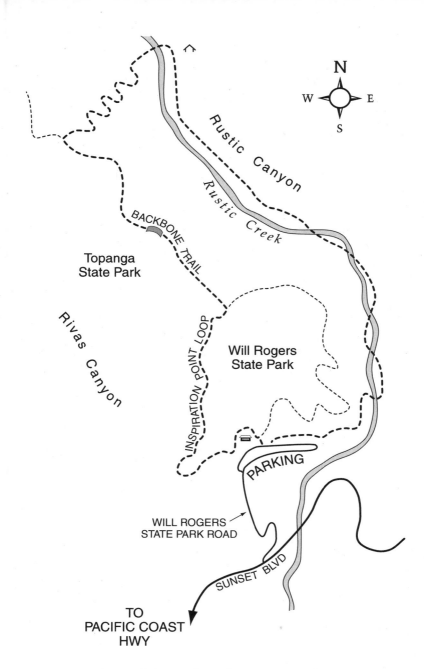

RUSTIC CANYON

Hike 32
Sullivan Canyon

Hiking distance: 7 miles round trip
Hiking time: 3.5 hours
Elevation gain: 400 feet
Maps: U.S.G.S. Topanga
   Trail Map of the Santa Monica Mountains East

Summary of hike: The hike up Sullivan Canyon parallels a seasonal creek through a shady canyon. Alive with the singing of birds, this hike sounds and feels like an aviary housed within huge stands of sycamore, oak, and willow trees. This near-level canyon is ideal for picnics.

Driving directions: From Santa Monica, drive north on the Pacific Coast Highway 1.6 miles to Chautauqua Boulevard and turn right. Continue 0.9 miles to Sunset Boulevard and turn right. Drive approximately 3 miles to Mandeville Canyon Road. Turn left on Mandeville Canyon Road, and turn left again at the first street—Westridge Road. Drive 1.2 miles on Westridge Road to Bayliss Road. Turn left on Bayliss Road, and drive 0.3 miles to Queensferry Road. Turn left and park at the gate.

Hiking directions: Step around the ominous-looking gate that closes off the road to motor vehicles. Walk down the short service road to the beginning of Sullivan Canyon. Go to the right, heading north along the graveled trail of the canyon floor. The near-level trail heads through narrow canyon walls past sandstone outcroppings. At 3.5 miles is a junction. Straight ahead, the north trail begins a serious ascent to Mulholland Drive; the left trail heads up the west ridge on a fire road. This junction is the turnaround spot. Return on the same trail.

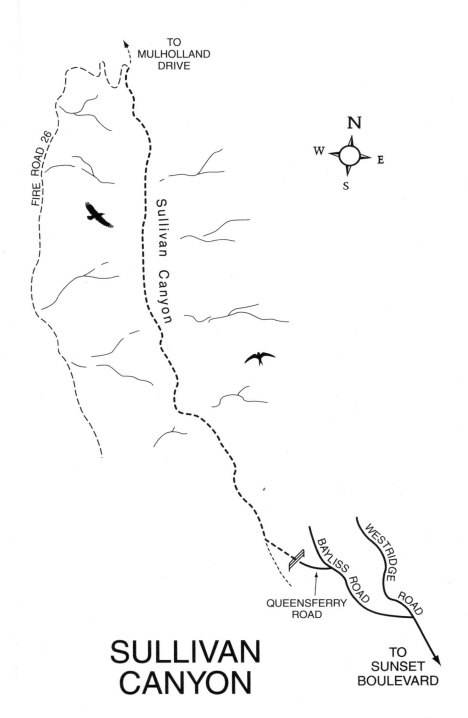

TO
MULHOLLAND
DRIVE

FIRE ROAD 26

Sullivan Canyon

N
W E
S

BAYLISS ROAD

WESTRIDGE ROAD

QUEENSFERRY
ROAD

TO
SUNSET
BOULEVARD

SULLIVAN
CANYON

Hike 33
The Venice Canals

Hiking distance: 1 mile or more
Hiking time: Variable
Elevation gain: Level
Maps: U.S.G.S. Venice
    City of Venice map

Summary of hike: The Venice Canals are a pastoral residential retreat. Six interwoven water canals flow through this charming neighborhood with walking paths beside the canals. Based on the canals of Venice, Italy, Abbott Kinney's "Venice of America" was completed in 1905. Landscaped walkways and diverse architecture make this walk an enchanting visual experience. Fourteen bridges and well-maintained walkways allow flexibility to walk around all six canals for any distance, direction, or length of time. Canoes, paddle boats, and ducks frequent the waterways.

Driving directions: The Venice Canals are located near the Pacific Coast between Washington Avenue and Venice Boulevard, only two blocks east of Pacific Avenue, which parallels the ocean. Dell Avenue crosses over the canals via four arched bridges. Park on Dell Avenue anywhere along the residential street.

Hiking directions: The canals have walking paths that border the water on each side. Fourteen bridges span the canals, connecting all the walkways. Choose your own path.
    One block west of the Grand Canal is Venice Beach and the Venice Boardwalk. The boardwalk parallels the ocean front from Washington Avenue for several miles north to the Santa Monica Pier.

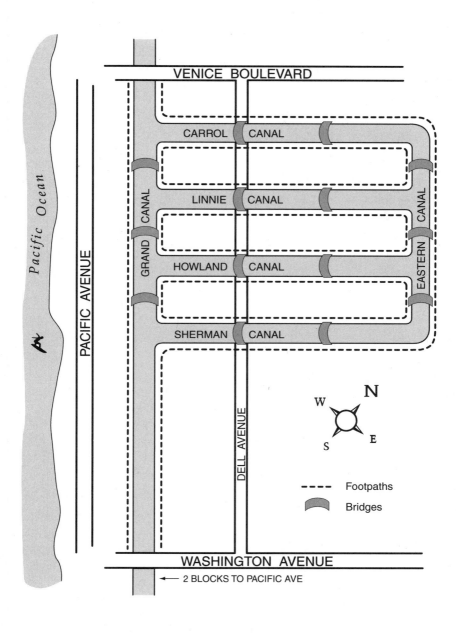

VENICE CANALS

Hike 34
Runyan Canyon Loop

Hiking distance: 2-mile loop
Hiking time: 1 hour
Elevation gain: 500 feet
Maps: U.S.G.S. Hollywood

Summary of hike: Runyan Canyon Park, a wildlife preserve, was purchased by the Santa Monica Mountains Conservancy and the City of Los Angeles in 1984. This trail loops around Runyan Canyon and crosses a broad gorge overlooking the canyon and the city. The trail passes the ruins of a pool house designed by Frank Lloyd Wright and lived in for several years by Errol Flynn. Remember, these are ruins, so use your imagination.

Driving directions: At the intersection of Franklin Avenue and Highland Avenue in Hollywood, drive 0.3 miles west on Franklin to Fuller Avenue and turn right. Continue 0.5 miles to The Pines gate at the end of the road. Park along the street wherever a space is available.

Hiking directions: From the parking area, walk through The Pines gate into Runyan Canyon Park at the end of Fuller Avenue. A short distance past the entrance is a trail to the left—the beginning of the loop. Take this trail as it curves along the chaparral-covered hillside parallel to the canyon floor. At one mile, near the head of Runyan Canyon, the trail circles over to the east side of the canyon. Watch for a narrow trail to the right heading back towards the south. This trail leads to Cloud's Rest, an exceptional overlook with 360-degree panoramic views. The trail continues to Inspiration Point and the Wright pool house ruins, then descends to the canyon floor and back to the trailhead.

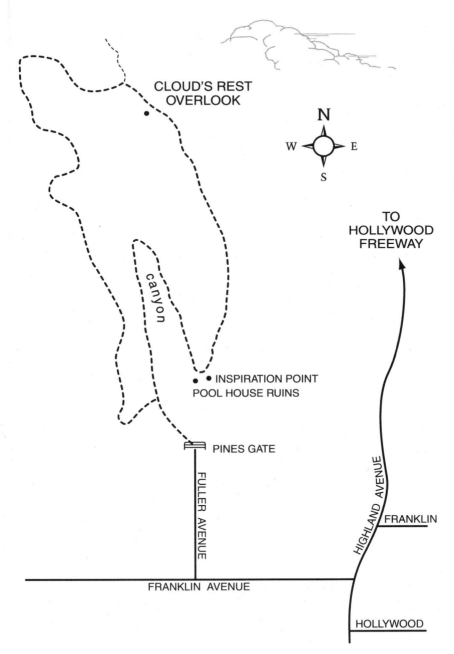

CLOUD'S REST
OVERLOOK

N
W　E
S

TO
HOLLYWOOD
FREEWAY

canyon

● INSPIRATION POINT
POOL HOUSE RUINS

PINES GATE

FULLER AVENUE

HIGHLAND AVENUE

FRANKLIN

FRANKLIN AVENUE

HOLLYWOOD

RUNYAN CANYON

Hike 35
Hollywood Reservoir

Open weekdays 6:30 — 10 a.m. and 2—5 p.m.
Open weekends 6:30 a.m.—5 p.m.

Hiking distance: 4-mile loop
Hiking time: 1.5 hours
Elevation gain: Level hiking
Maps: U.S.G.S. Hollywood and Burbank

Summary of hike: This hike follows the perimeter of the Hollywood Reservoir on an asphalt service road that is closed to vehicles. The road, which is landscaped on both sides, is a rural retreat inside the city that is frequently used as a walking and jogging trail. The tall foliage obscures full views of the reservoir except when crossing Mulholland Dam. The dam crossing is magnificent. To the north is Mount Lee and the "Hollywood" sign overlooking the beautiful reservoir below. To the south is a view of Hollywood and the Los Angeles Basin.

Driving directions: From Hollywood, take Highland Avenue north past the Hollywood Bowl, curving left onto Cahuenga Boulevard. Continue one mile to Barham Boulevard. Turn right and cross over the Hollywood Freeway. Drive 0.2 miles to Lake Hollywood Drive and turn right.

From the Hollywood Freeway/101, take the Barham Boulevard Exit, and head north 0.2 miles to Lake Hollywood Drive. Turn right.

Follow the winding Lake Hollywood Drive through a residential neighborhood for 0.8 miles to the Hollywood Reservoir entrance gate on the right. Park alongside the road.

Hiking directions From the parking area, the reservoir entrance is on the right (south). The paved path follows the perimeter of the reservoir through the shaded pine forest. At the south end of the reservoir, cross Mulholland Dam. After crossing, the path loops north to Tahoe Drive. Bear left along the road, returning to the parking area.

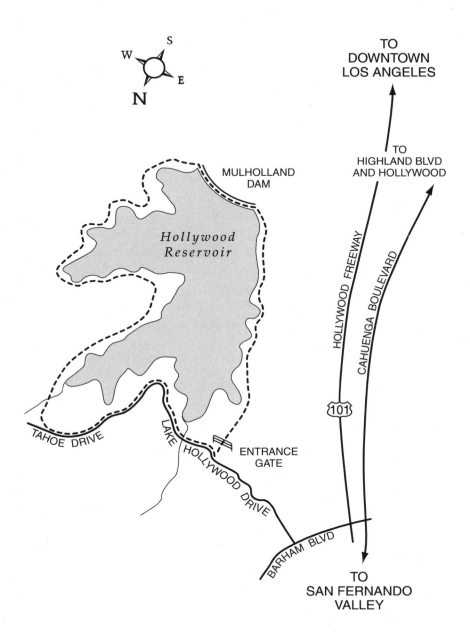

HOLLYWOOD RESERVOIR

Hike 36
Mount Lee
and the "Hollywood" sign

Hiking distance: 3 miles round trip
Hiking time: 1.5 hours
Elevation gain: 550 feet
Maps: U.S.G.S. Hollywood and Burbank

Summary of hike: This trail leads to the famous "HOLLY-WOOD" sign on Mount Lee. The sign was originally built in the 1920s to read "HOLLYWOODLAND," promoting real estate development in Beachwood Canyon. In 1978, entertainment celebrities donated money to replace the original sign, which was worn from time, weather, and vandalism. The sign now measures 50 feet high by 450 feet long. It sits just below the Mount Lee summit. Although the sign itself is fenced off from direct visitation, the views from atop Mount Lee are superb.

Driving directions: At the intersection of Franklin Avenue and Western Avenue in Hollywood, drive 0.7 miles west on Franklin Avenue to Beachwood Drive and turn right (north). Continue 1.7 miles up Beachwood Drive to Hollyridge Drive. Park near this intersection.

Hiking directions: From the intersection, hike up Hollyridge Drive 200 feet to the trailhead on the left. From the Hollyridge Trail, the "HOLLYWOOD" sign looms over the landscape. Follow the ridge northeast, overlooking the Sunset Horse Ranch on the left. Continue 0.5 miles to an intersection with the unmarked Mulholland Trail. Take a sharp left up this trail as it heads west on a fire road to Mount Lee Drive 0.3 miles ahead. At Mount Lee Drive, the left fork leads downhill to excellent frontal views of the sign. The right fork heads uphill to the ridge above and behind the sign, overlooking Burbank and the San Fernando Valley. Return along the same path.

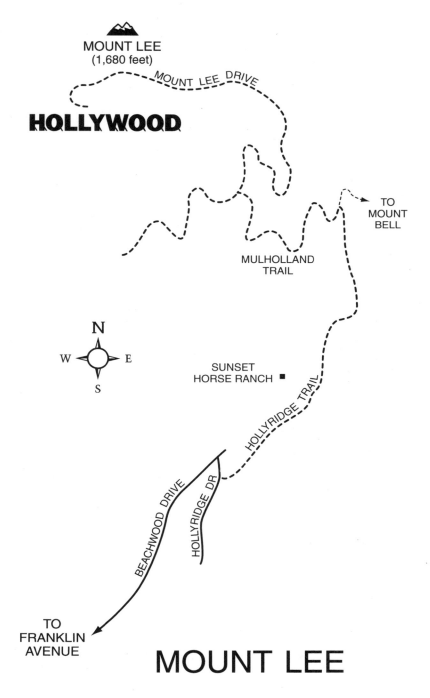

MOUNT LEE
(1,680 feet)

MOUNT LEE DRIVE

HOLLYWOOD

TO
MOUNT
BELL

MULHOLLAND
TRAIL

N
W E
S

SUNSET
HORSE RANCH ■

HOLLYRIDGE TRAIL

BEACHWOOD DRIVE

HOLLYRIDGE DR

TO
FRANKLIN
AVENUE

MOUNT LEE

Hike 37
Bronson Caves

Hiking distance: 0.6 miles round trip
Hiking time: 0.5 hours
Elevation gain: 40 feet
Maps: U.S.G.S. Hollywood
Hileman's Recreational/Geological Map of Griffith Park

Summary of hike: At the southwest corner of Griffith Park is a fun, short hike to one of Hollywood's most frequently filmed caves. Originally a quarry, the crushed rock from the caves was used to pave the streets of a growing Hollywood. Many western and science fiction movie producers have shot on location at these manmade caves. *Star Trek, Mission Impossible, Gunsmoke, Bonanza,* and the *Batman and Robin* series have been filmed here.

Driving directions: At the intersection of Hollywood Boulevard and Western Avenue in Hollywood, drive 0.5 miles west on Hollywood Boulevard to Bronson Avenue. Turn right and continue 1.5 miles on Bronson Avenue (which merges with Canyon Drive) past Bronson Park to the end of the road. Park in the lot on the left.

Hiking directions: From the parking lot, hike back along the park road 100 feet to the trailhead on the left (east) side of the road. The trail gently climbs a quarter mile to the caves. From here you may walk through the caves and around the hill. Return along the same path.

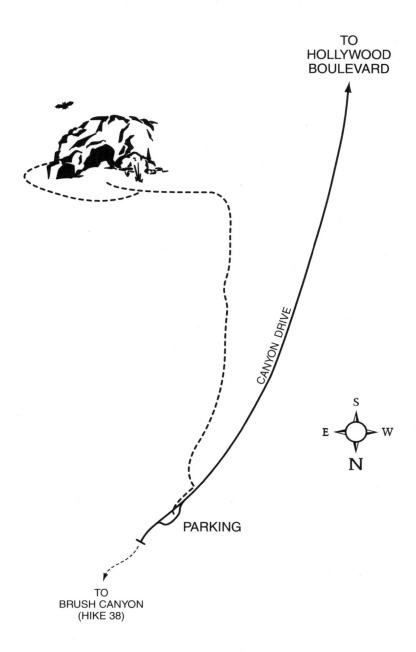

TO
HOLLYWOOD
BOULEVARD

CANYON DRIVE

S

E ✦ W

N

PARKING

TO
BRUSH CANYON
(HIKE 38)

BRONSON CAVES

Hike 38
Brush Canyon

Hiking distance: 2 miles round trip
Hiking time: 1 hour
Elevation gain: 500 feet
Maps: U.S.G.S. Hollywood and Burbank
      Hileman's Recreational/Geological Map of Griffith Park

Summary of hike: Brush Canyon is a beautiful yet lightly traveled trail in Griffith Park. The hike begins in a forest of sycamore and oak trees. The trail climbs into a drier chaparral and shrub terrain in the undeveloped mountainous interior of the park. From the top are views of secluded canyons, Hollywood, and the Los Angeles Basin.

Driving directions: At the intersection of Hollywood Boulevard and Western Avenue in Hollywood, drive 0.5 miles west on Hollywood Boulevard to Bronson Avenue. Turn right and continue 1.5 miles on Bronson Avenue (which merges with Canyon Drive) past Bronson Park to the end of the road. Park in the lot on the left.

Hiking directions: From the parking lot, hike uphill to the north past the vehicle gate. Continue on the fire road past the Pacific Electric quarry. At 0.25 miles is an expansive park and picnic area. After passing the park, the trail begins to climb, leaving the shade of the trees for the drought-resistant shrubs. Continue 0.75 miles to the Mullholland Trail junction. Take the trail to the right another quarter mile to Mount Hollywood Drive. From Mount Hollywood Drive, retrace your steps back to the parking lot.

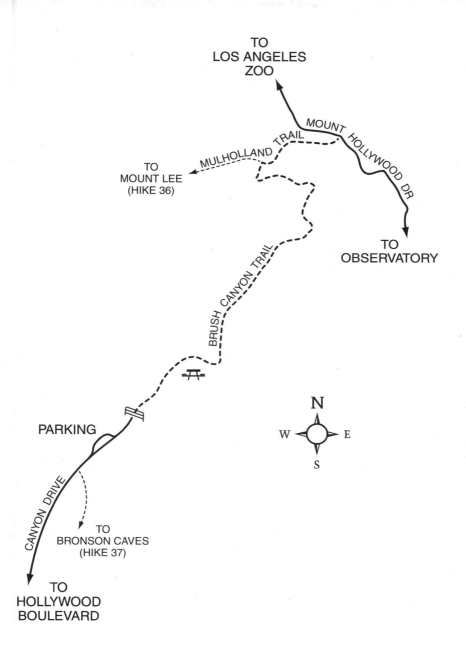

TO
LOS ANGELES
ZOO

MOUNT HOLLYWOOD DR

MULHOLLAND TRAIL

TO
MOUNT LEE
(HIKE 36)

TO
OBSERVATORY

BRUSH CANYON TRAIL

PARKING

N

W E

S

CANYON DRIVE

TO
BRONSON CAVES
(HIKE 37)

TO
HOLLYWOOD
BOULEVARD

BRUSH CANYON

Hike 39
Griffith Park Observatory
to Ferndell Park

Hiking distance: 2.5 miles round trip
Hiking time: 1.5 hours
Elevation gain: 500 feet
Maps: U.S.G.S. Hollywood
Hileman's Recreational/Geological Map of Griffith Park

Summary of hike: This hike offers panoramic views of the Los Angeles area from the ocean to the San Gabriel Mountains. The garden pathways of Ferndell Park follow along a stream lined with moss-covered rocks. Charming footbridges cross the stream.

The hike begins at the copper-domed Griffith Park Observatory. The observatory has planetarium and laser programs, a gift shop, and various science displays. An observation deck with telescopes winds around the south side of this architectural landmark.

Driving directions: From Los Feliz Boulevard in Hollywood, there are two ways to arrive at the trailhead parking lot. You may take Fern Dell Drive north 2.3 miles to the Griffith Park Observatory parking lot. Or, take Vermont Avenue north 1.8 miles to the observatory parking lot. Both directions offer a beautiful, curving drive through Griffith Park.

Hiking directions: From the parking lot, walk towards the observatory. Take the trail to the left (east) of the observatory for 0.25 miles to an overlook and trail junction. Take the right trail another 0.25 miles to the next junction. Take either the Lower Trail (the shorter route) or the Upper Trail, and continue down to Ferndell Park. Stroll along the quarter-mile path, meandering along the park's year-round stream, over bridges, past waterfalls and pools, and through the lush gardens and glen. To return, retrace your steps back to the parking lot, taking either the Upper or Lower Trail on the way back.

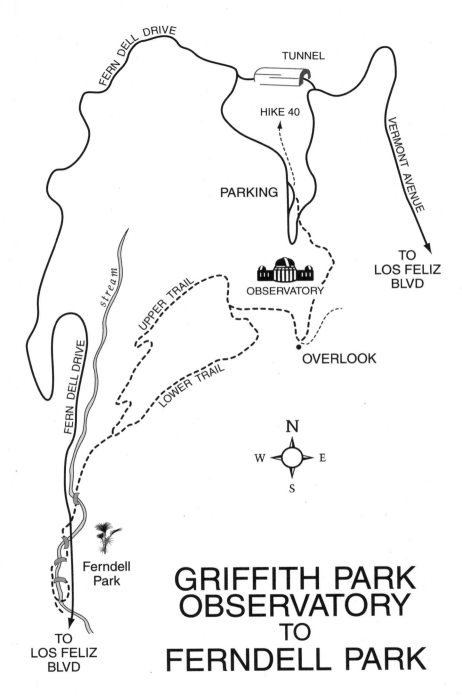

FERN DELL DRIVE

TUNNEL

HIKE 40

VERMONT AVENUE

PARKING

TO
LOS FELIZ
BLVD

OBSERVATORY

stream

UPPER TRAIL

LOWER TRAIL

FERN DELL DRIVE

OVERLOOK

N
W · E
S

Ferndell
Park

GRIFFITH PARK
OBSERVATORY
TO
FERNDELL PARK

TO
LOS FELIZ
BLVD

Hike 40
Mount Hollywood Trail
and Dante's View

Hiking distance: 3 miles round trip
Hiking time: 1.5 hours
Elevation gain: 500 feet
Maps: U.S.G.S. Hollywood and Burbank
Hileman's Recreational/Geological Map of Griffith Park

Summary of hike: The Mount Hollywood Trail takes you to the top of Mount Hollywood and offers commanding views of the San Fernando Valley, the Los Angeles Basin, and the San Gabriel Mountains. The trail also includes Dante's View, a terraced two-acre garden planted by Dante Orgolini in the 1960s. This south-facing garden has picnic benches and shade trees along its intertwining trail.

The hike begins near the Griffith Park Observatory. The observatory, which opened in 1935, has excellent science exhibits and planetarium shows.

Driving directions: Follow the same driving directions as Hike 39 to the Griffith Park Observatory parking lot.

Hiking directions: From the parking lot, hike north (in the opposite direction of the observatory) to the well-marked Mount Hollywood trailhead. A short distance later, you will pass the Berlin Forest, a friendship park between the people of Berlin and Los Angeles. There are wonderful views and benches where you can relax before continuing. At 0.75 miles, a junction indicates the beginning of the loop. The trail to the right is the shortest route to Dante's View and a joy to stroll along. After the garden, continue on the main trail as it curves around the hillside, opening up to views of the San Fernando Valley and the surrounding mountains. A short trail to the left leads to a lookout at the top of Mount Hollywood. After enjoying the views, go back to the main trail and continue to the left, completing the loop and returning to the parking lot.

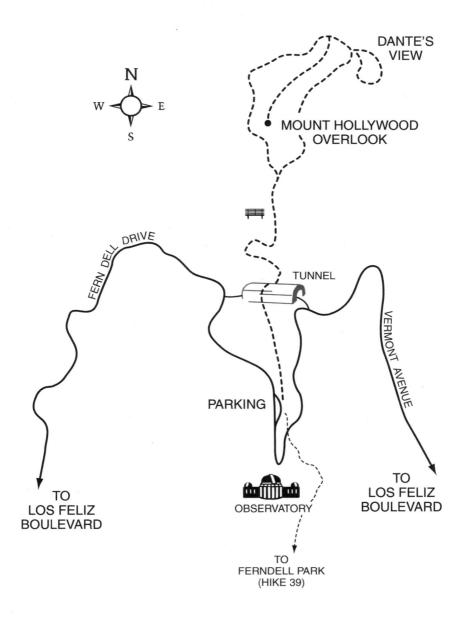

N
W · E
S

DANTE'S VIEW

MOUNT HOLLYWOOD OVERLOOK

FERN DELL DRIVE

TUNNEL

VERMONT AVENUE

PARKING

TO LOS FELIZ BOULEVARD

OBSERVATORY

TO LOS FELIZ BOULEVARD

TO FERNDELL PARK (HIKE 39)

MOUNT HOLLYWOOD

Hike 41
Bird Sanctuary Loop

Hiking distance: 0.5-mile loop
Hiking time: 0.5 hours
Elevation gain: Level hiking
Maps: U.S.G.S. Hollywood and Burbank
Hileman's Recreational/Geological Map of Griffith Park

Summary of hike: The bird sanctuary loop is a short hike through a pastoral wooded glen. The trail is shaded by large eucalyptus and pine trees. A stream flows through the lush glen, and a footbridge crosses over the stream by a pond. Beautiful rock walls line the pathways.

Driving directions: At the intersection of Los Feliz Boulevard and Vermont Avenue in Hollywood, drive one mile north on Vermont Avenue past the Greek Theater to the bird sanctuary on the right side of the road. (The Griffith Park Observatory is 0.8 miles further.)

Hiking directions: From the parking area, walk to the right past the "Bird Sanctuary" sign. This well-defined trail heads north through the sanctuary and loops back to the trailhead.
A narrow footpath leads through the forest on the hillside above the east side of the sanctuary, parallel to the main path.

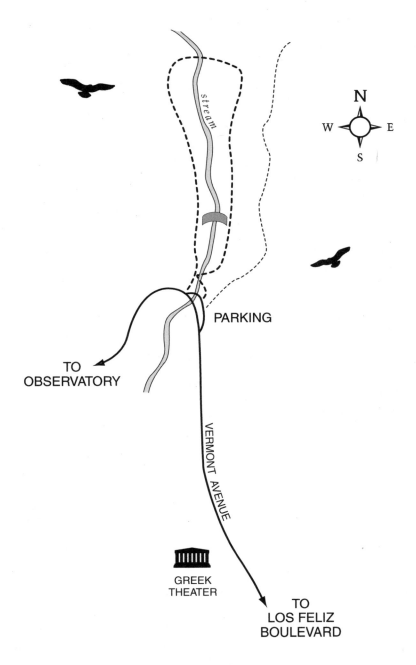

TO
OBSERVATORY

PARKING

VERMONT AVENUE

GREEK
THEATER

TO
LOS FELIZ
BOULEVARD

BIRD SANCTUARY

Hike 42
Beacon Hill

Hiking distance: 2.5 miles to 4 miles
Hiking time: 1.5 hours to 2 hours
Elevation gain: 550 feet
Maps: U.S.G.S. Burbank
        Hileman's Recreational/Geological Map of Griffith Park

Summary of hike: Beacon Hill is the easternmost hill of the 50-mile long Santa Monica Mountain Range. An illuminated beacon once resided on the top of Beacon Hill, warning aircraft of the mountains next to the Glendale Grand Central Airport, the main airport for Los Angeles and Hollywood during the 1910s and 1920s. From Beacon Hill you can see it all—from the ocean to the mountains and everything inbetween.

Driving directions: Start from the intersection of Los Feliz Boulevard and Crystal Springs Drive in Hollywood, located in the southeast area of Griffith Park. To arrive at this intersection from the Golden State Freeway/I-5, take the Los Feliz Boulevard Exit. Drive west a short distance to Crystal Springs Drive.

Drive north on Crystal Springs Drive for 1.3 miles to the merry-go-round turnoff on the left. Turn left and park in the first parking lot.

Hiking directions: From the parking lot, walk back across the road and uphill to the right for 100 yards to a junction. Take the trail to the left, heading uphill to the Fern Canyon Trail. Continue on the Fern Canyon Trail as it winds around the hillside. At one mile is a five-way trail junction and benches. The trail to the left leads 0.25 miles to Beacon Hill. After taking in the views from Beacon Hill, return to the junction. For a 2.5-mile round trip hike, return along the same trail back to the parking lot. To make a four-mile loop, take the left trail (Coolidge Trail), and continue one mile to a fork in the trail. Take the left fork (Lower Beacon Trail), and return to the parking lot.

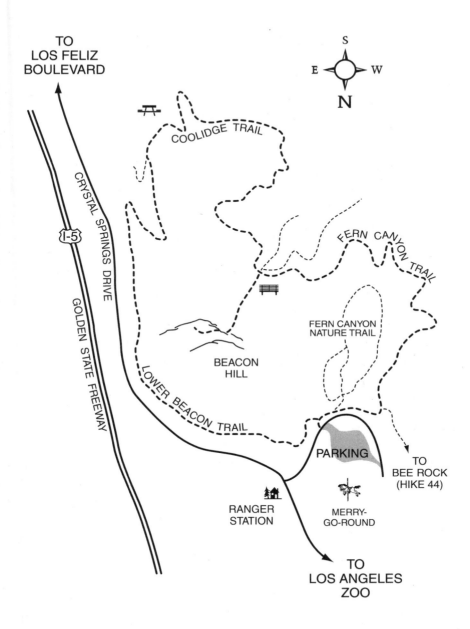

TO
LOS FELIZ
BOULEVARD

S
E ← ☀ → W
N

COOLIDGE TRAIL

CRYSTAL SPRINGS DRIVE

I-5

FERN CANYON TRAIL

GOLDEN STATE FREEWAY

LOWER BEACON TRAIL

BEACON
HILL

FERN CANYON
NATURE TRAIL

PARKING

TO
BEE ROCK
(HIKE 44)

RANGER
STATION

MERRY-
GO-ROUND

TO
LOS ANGELES
ZOO

BEACON HILL

Hike 43
Fern Canyon Nature Trail

Hiking distance: 0.6-mile loop
Hiking time: 0.5 hours
Elevation gain: 150 feet
Maps: U.S.G.S. Burbank
        Hileman's Recreational/Geological Map of Griffith Park

Summary of hike: The Fern Canyon Nature Trail takes you through a forested area along various looping trails. The paths cross footbridges and lead to a natural amphitheater. This nature walk is located just minutes from the merry-go-round and the Old Zoo Park.

Driving directions: Start from the intersection of Los Feliz Boulevard and Crystal Springs Drive in Hollywood, located in the southeast area of Griffith Park. To arrive at this intersection from the Golden State Freeway/I-5, take the Los Feliz Boulevard Exit. Drive west a short distance to Crystal Springs Drive.
    Drive north on Crystal Springs Drive for 1.3 miles to the merry-go-round turnoff on the left. Turn left and park in the first parking lot.

Hiking directions: From the parking lot, walk back across the road and uphill to the right for about 100 yards to a trail junction. Just before the junction is the Fern Canyon Nature Trail with a large sign. All of the trails interconnect and loop back to the entrance. Choose your own path.

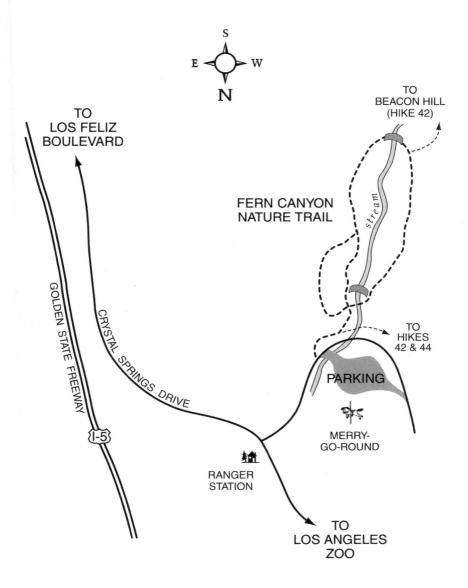

FERN CANYON
NATURE TRAIL

Hike 44
Old Zoo Trail
and Bee Rock

Hiking distance: 2.2-mile loop
Hiking time: 1.5 hours
Elevation gain: 300 feet
Maps: U.S.G.S. Burbank
　　　　Hileman's Recreational/Geological Map of Griffith Park

Summary of hike: This is a wonderful trail to a large sandstone outcropping in the shape of a beehive called Bee Rock. There are great.views of Griffith Park. The trail returns through the old Los Angeles Zoo along its walking paths, expansive lawns, and abandoned animal cages.

Driving directions: Start from the intersection of Los Feliz Boulevard and Crystal Springs Drive in Hollywood, located in the southeast area of Griffith Park. To arrive at this intersection from the Golden State Freeway/I-5, take the Los Feliz Boulevard Exit. Drive west a short distance to Crystal Springs Drive.

Drive north on Crystal Springs Drive for 1.3 miles to the merry-go-round turnoff on the left. Turn left and park in the first parking lot.

Hiking directions: From the parking lot, walk back across the road and uphill to the right for 100 yards to a trail junction. Take the Old Zoo Trail to the right, heading uphill into the trees. (The trail to the left goes to Beacon Hill, Hike 42.) At 0.5 miles, Bee Rock comes into view. Another 0.25 miles is the Bee Rock Trail to the left. On the right is the return route through the old zoo. First, take the trail to Bee Rock. The final ascent up to Bee Rock is steep, but the views make it worth the effort.

After descending back to the junction, go through the gate and down along the paths of the old zoo, which has been converted into a park. The paths lead back to the merry-go-round and the parking lot, completing the loop.

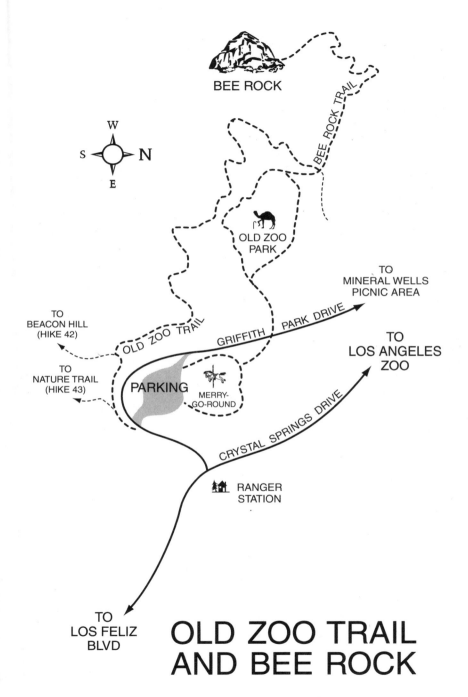

BEE ROCK

BEE ROCK TRAIL

W
S — N
E

OLD ZOO
PARK

TO
MINERAL WELLS
PICNIC AREA

TO
BEACON HILL
(HIKE 42)

OLD ZOO TRAIL

GRIFFITH PARK DRIVE

TO
LOS ANGELES
ZOO

TO
NATURE TRAIL
(HIKE 43)

PARKING

MERRY-
GO-ROUND

CRYSTAL SPRINGS DRIVE

RANGER
STATION

TO
LOS FELIZ
BLVD

OLD ZOO TRAIL
AND BEE ROCK

Hike 45
Amir's Garden

Hiking distance: 1 mile round trip
Hiking time: 1 hour
Elevation gain: 300 feet
Maps: U.S.G.S. Burbank
      Hileman's Recreational/Geological Map of Griffith Park

Summary of hike: Amir's Garden is a beautifully landscaped hillside with rock-lined paths, benches, and picnic tables on several layers of terraces. There is a wonderful network of trails and stairways leading through the garden. The garden was created in 1971 by Amir Dialameh, who designed, planted, nurtured, and maintained this two-acre Eden.

Driving directions: Start from the intersection of Los Feliz Boulevard and Crystal Springs Drive in Hollywood, located in the southeast area of Griffith Park. To arrive at this intersection from the Golden State Freeway/I-5, take the Los Feliz Boulevard Exit. Drive west a short distance to Crystal Springs Drive.

    Continue 1.5 miles to Griffith Park Drive (just past the merry-go-round) and turn left. Drive 1.3 miles to the Mineral Wells Picnic Area and park.

Hiking directions: From the parking area at the lower south end of Mineral Wells Picnic Area, take the trail west to a three-way junction, immediately ahead. Follow the middle fork up towards the water tank. A half mile ahead is a lookout and a sharp trail switchback. Amir's Garden is at this lookout point. The garden paths zigzag across the hillside. After strolling and enjoying the garden, return along the same path.

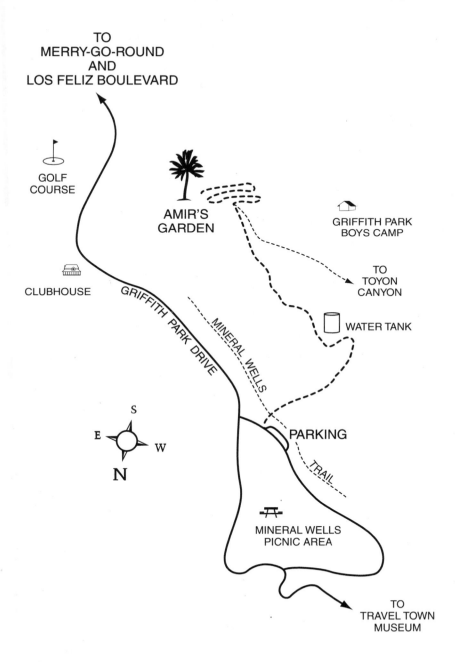

TO
MERRY-GO-ROUND
AND
LOS FELIZ BOULEVARD

GOLF
COURSE

AMIR'S
GARDEN

GRIFFITH PARK
BOYS CAMP

CLUBHOUSE

TO
TOYON
CANYON

GRIFFITH PARK DRIVE

MINERAL WELLS

WATER TANK

S

E   W

N

PARKING

TRAIL

MINERAL WELLS
PICNIC AREA

TO
TRAVEL TOWN
MUSEUM

AMIR'S GARDEN

Other Day Hike Guidebooks

Day Hikes on Oahu $9.95

Day Hikes on Maui. 8.95

Day Hikes on Kauai 8.95

Day Hikes in Yosemite National Park. 8.95

Day Hikes Around Lake Tahoe 8.95

Day Hikes Around Los Angeles 11.95

Day Hikes in Ventura County, California. 11.95

Day Hikes Around Santa Barbara, California 11.95

Day Hikes in San Luis Obispo County, California 14.95

Day Hikes in Aspen, Colorado 7.95

Day Hikes in Boulder, Colorado. 8.95

Day Hikes in Steamboat Springs, Colorado. 8.95

Day Hikes in Summit County, Colorado 8.95

Day Hikes in Yellowstone National Park. 9.95

Day Hikes in Grand Teton National Park and Jackson Hole . . . 8.95

Day Hikes in the Beartooth Mountains
  Red Lodge, Montana to Yellowstone National Park. 8.95

Day Hikes Around Bozeman, Montana 9.95

Day Hikes Around Missoula, Montana 9.95

Day Hikes in Sedona, Arizona 9.95

Day Trips on St. Martin 9.95

These books may be purchased at your local bookstore or
outdoor shop. Or, order them direct from the distributor:

The Globe Pequot Press
P.O. Box 833 · Old Saybrook, CT 06475
www.globe-pequot.com

1-800-243-0495

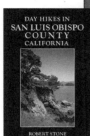

DAY HIKES IN
SAN LUIS OBISPO
COUNTY
CALIFORNIA

ROBERT STONE

DAY HIKES AROUND
SANTA
BARBARA
CALIFORNIA

46 OF THE BEST
ROBERT STONE

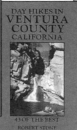

DAY HIKES IN
VENTURA
COUNTY
CALIFORNIA

43 OF THE BEST
ROBERT STONE

DAY HIKES AROUND
LOS ANGELES

45 GREAT HIKES
ROBERT STONE

DAY HIKES IN
YOSEMITE
NATIONAL PARK

25 FAVORITE HIKES
ROBERT STONE

DAY HIKES AROUND
LAKE
TAHOE

ROBERT STONE

DAY HIKES ON
OAHU

ROBERT STONE

DAY HIKES ON
MAUI

ROBERT STONE

DAY HIKES ON
KAUAI

ROBERT STONE

DAY HIKES IN
SEDONA
ARIZONA

25 FAVORITE HIKES
ROBERT STONE

DAY HIKES IN
YELLOWSTONE
NATIONAL PARK

54 GREAT HIKES
ROBERT STONE

DAY HIKES IN
GRAND TETON
NATIONAL PARK
AND
JACKSON HOLE

ROBERT STONE

DAY HIKES IN
SUMMIT
COUNTY
COLORADO

ROBERT STONE

DAY HIKES IN
BOULDER
COLORADO

ROBERT STONE

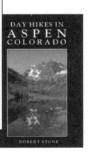

DAY HIKES IN
ASPEN
COLORADO

ROBERT STONE

DAY HIKES IN
STEAMBOAT
SPRINGS
COLORADO

ROBERT STONE

DAY HIKES AROUND
MISSOULA
MONTANA

INCLUDING THE BITTERROOTS
AND THE SEELEY-SWAN VALLEY
ROBERT STONE

DAY HIKES AROUND
BOZEMAN
MONTANA

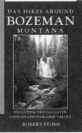

INCLUDING THE GALLATIN
CANYON AND PARADISE VALLEY
ROBERT STONE

DAY HIKES IN THE
BEARTOOTH
MOUNTAINS

RED LODGE, MONTANA TO
YELLOWSTONE NATIONAL PARK
ROBERT STONE

DAY TRIPS ON
ST. MARTIN

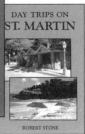

ROBERT STONE

Notes